Unshakable

A Girl's Guide to Standing Firm When Everyone Around You is Falling

Tai Sophia

Contents

Preface

What's a girl to do? She wants to be included and accepted, loved and even admired. She wants to dream big and accomplish great things. She wants to live a life that she can look back upon with satisfaction and joy, knowing she lived it to the fullest. But, like gravity, there's this ever-present force that seeks to keep her grounded....in self-absorption, deception, idolatry, vanity, self-righteousness, bitterness, worldliness and the list goes on, unique to each individual. The things she wants to do she cannot do and things she doesn't want to do, these she does. Everything just seems....hard.

Well, God *has* called us to be more than conquerors, victorious and full of joy, living abundantly and purposefully with a vision far greater than ourselves. And He doesn't call us to it and then leave us stranded. God has graciously equipped us with everything we need to live a life of magnitude and impact, but there has to be some 'first things first' settled in our hearts. That is where this book comes in.

With the wisdom of experience and hard-fought battles under her belt, Tai Sophia shares her heart to encourage her fellow women-in-arms to aspire to a calling that surpasses all she can ask or think and breaks free from the downward pull of worldliness and sin. The sky really is the limit when we pursue our dreams in the light of truth from the Giver of Truth. The Captain of our Souls, Jesus Christ, just stands ready and waiting to send us out into the world with purposes He designed specifically for each one of us from before the foundation of the world!

So, if you're feeling the upward tug away from the pull of this world and would like to be propelled into the adventure of faith-based life, above the shackles and confines of self-centered, idolatrous living, this book will lead you to a place where you can take that stance of allegiance to Christ with confidence and implicit trust, flight cap in hand, ready to go wherever He leads.

Tai has truly walked out everything she writes about here. She shares her struggles transparently with you and in so doing, shows you that the battles can be won. I personally have watched her stand against friction, turbulence and

2

air pocketsof all sizes through the years (sometimes from her own deceitful heart), and have given glory to God for calling her heart to seek Him first and foremost in every situation. She has always broken free from the bonds of earth, buckled in to the Word of God, and come to a place of humble reckoning between truth and lies. Every morning, without fail, this girl was in her Bible – even if it was just a 'form of godliness' for a season – it was a discipline. And with discipline is where the victory is won. So girls, I tell you all this to just say, Tai is the real deal. The lifestyle portrayed in this book is indeed possible – it's not just talk, it's Tai's wholehearted walk.

Carin Polczynski, Tai's mother

Introduction

"For the moment all discipline seems painful rather than pleasant, but later it yields the peaceful fruit of righteousness to those who have been trained by it. Therefore lift your drooping hands and strengthen your weak knees, and make straight paths for your feet, so that what is lame may not be put out of joint but rather be healed." Hebrews 12:11-13

I was praying the other day about all of you young ladies and girls whom I meet all across Canada and the USA, and about the problem that I don't have the time to really get to know you and hear your hearts and tell you all that I wish I could about the important aspects of living in a way that is pleasing to the Lord and escaping the snares of the devil, because I'm just one girl – a pretty busy one at that – and I only have the same number of hours in a day as anyone else. I was also thinking about how many of you I see but never even have the chance to meet or talk to, and I was wishing that there was *some* way I could communicate to you how important you are to me, and how important your soul is to the Lord…and that there was *some* way I could just scoop you each up and take you out for tea or coffee…or just to hang out and talk, because there is just *so* much I wish I could talk to you about. There are so many lies in our world today aimed at you girls, and the devil does everything he can to keep you from a vibrant, joy-filled, victorious relationship with Jesus, and I was just wishing I could share some of the lessons I've learned with you, so that you, too, would have the chance to escape going down the lifeless road that *so* many girls go down these days. I long for you to come alive in Christ, to love Him more than anything else, and to escape the fires of spiritual death *before* they touch you.

So this book isn't anything particularly eloquent or astounding theologically…but it is a collection of everything that I long for you to know – really *know* – and I pray that what you read here will draw your heart closer to the Lord, and that it will cause you to live your life to please only Jesus, without a care of what the rest of the world thinks or says or does to try to stop you.

I've arranged my thoughts as a series of letters, so that it's a little more personal than just any old book…because it *is* personal. Not only is this written just for you (and I would have written it if you were the only one to read it), but I want you to take everything I say personally…and not to be thinking about how your friend so-and-so needs to change, but to be thinking about how *you* can apply what God teaches you through this book. What you do now is a matter of life or death…and that thought alone should cause you to take this all to heart. This book is not going to boost your self-esteem, or be a collection of nice, fluffy thoughts. No. What I write here leaves you with the responsibility to *do* something…and it might be uncomfortable- to change maybe the way you've always thought or heard things, perhaps to change the plans you thought you had all laid out for your future, to change the way you use your time, or even to change the way you talk or act or dress. You may discover that some things you thought were important are actually worthless (which may be especially hard for those of you whose lives are completely wrapped up in them – but Jesus will help you be free of them if you ask Him) and that some things which you thought were worthless are actually essential. Some of the things I say may be hard to take…but ask the Lord to help you understand, because I know He will. Some of the things He's been teaching me *are* hard to take at first, but they are the pavement to the road that leads to abundance of life in Christ, and as you practice them, they bring joy, and peace, and blessing from the Lord. And, I desire for you to walk on this road, as if you were my very own sister.

The verse I've quoted above is one I want you to keep in mind as you read this book, because, though some of what I say will be hard to hear, if you take it seriously, and begin to act on it, it will cause your life to bring forth beautiful fruit. The things I share will be like a map for you, so that you will be able to blaze straight and solid paths to walk on all throughout your life, so that you won't continue to be hurt and struggling through life, only barely surviving, and just getting worse and worse, but so that you can walk through life completely healed and set free of the disease of sin, and help others along too!

Now, let's begin…

Letter 1:

Broken Down

Dear Every-girl,

For, that is what I will call you – *Every-girl* – because these letters are to every girl who has ever desired to be closer to the Lord, and every girl who has desired to be His child, and every girl who wants to escape from the emptiness that most people (even many who call themselves Christians) live in – an emptiness which comes from *not* loving the Lord and His commands *above all else.*

Before you go any further in reading this book, I want you to stop reading when you get to the end of this sentence, close your eyes, and ask Jesus to teach you what He wants you to learn, and to help you to understand the truth, and to apply what you read to your life.

Now, I'm going to write this assuming that you have already prayed to give your life to Jesus, and asked Him to be your master, and to forgive all your sins. If you haven't, then skip to the last letter of this book, because this is the most important thing you could ever do, and just believing what your parents say isn't enough, and just trying to be good isn't enough. The *only* way you can be saved from your sins and ever hope to live in a way that is pleasing to the Lord is through His strength, because, on our own, we are far too weak and full of imperfection to ever be pleasing in the sight of a completely perfect and holy God. (Just pause there for a minute and think about what it really means that God is "perfect" and "holy". Chances are, you've heard that before…maybe even a lot of times, but have never really actually stopped to think about what it means, and how that knowledge should affect your own life.) And even if you *have* prayed to become a Christian, you may need to hear that, because some people mistakenly believe that we can do all these good things to make God love us more. But that is simply not true. We can't do anything in our own strength to please the Lord. It's like a 2-year-old trying to make cookies for her mom.

The 2-year-old is only going to make an big mess if she tries to make cookies on her own; she doesn't know how ingredients work together – or even what they *are* – and she doesn't yet have the strength to mix them together on her own. But if she asks her mom if she can help, her mom will tell her exact and useful things that she can do, that will actually end up helping, because her mom knows all about making cookies and has the whole process already planned out in her head, and she can even lift up the 2-year-old and help her to stir everything together in a big bowl, so that the 2-year-old has fun, and actually feels like she is doing something useful, even though her mom might have to make some slight adjustments and keep close watch of the little girl so that everything comes out alright. In a somewhat similar, though much more real and important way, it is only when we humbly come to Jesus and admit that we can't do it on our own that He lifts us up, and helps us to do things that are pleasing to Him – and then rewards us for obeying Him, as if we actually did something good, though we ought to know that we couldn't have done it or even *wanted* to do it unless Jesus was helping us, because I am afraid that we are simply born sinners, and our sinfulness is what we naturally tend to do, just like a baby naturally makes a mess of things that are in its reach.

That leads me to one of the most important things we all must do: We need to be able to humbly come before the Lord, and ask Him to show us our own sin, and how we have broken His laws and caused Him pain, and how we have been displeasing to him. And then, you must be able to confess those things to Him- to admit that you've done them, and then to ask for His forgiveness, and ask Him to take all those things away, and to cleanse you, and to help you to run from them, and not to go back to them again. And this should be something that we do, not just once, but every day, because sin creeps in all the time, and causes our hearts to be blackened, and we need to come before the Lord and ask Him to clean all those things out of us often, so that we can have pure hearts before him. Matthew 5:8 says, *"Blessed are the pure in heart, for they shall see God."* What an amazing promise!

There was a point, not all that long ago, when I thought I was doing really well spiritually, mainly because I didn't *see* any sin in my life, and so that obviously meant that I was being a good Christian...right? Well...that or I was just a blind Christian. And I was most certainly walking around blind to my sin. When we are walking with the Lord as we should be, we can see our sin more and more clearly as we look upon His glory and see His holiness more and more clearly. If we can't see any sin in our lives, an alarm system should start going off in our heads, because this may mean (and, in my case, was true) that we not only are not perfect as we appear to ourselves to be, but may actually have our spiritual "glasses" gunked up with pride. I had gotten into a rut of comparing myself with other sinful people, and thinking that I was oh-so-wonderful compared to them...and I neglected to measure myself with *the Lord's standards* of complete holiness. I must say that the results of those 2 measuring systems are very dramatically different, and even when you are doing really well compared with other people, you are probably still failing to live up to *God's* standard in many different ways.

God decided to show me one day just how far I had fallen from living a life that was pleasing to Him, and I'm going to share what I wrote in my journal that day with you(which I then posted on my blog: www.beggarlybouquet.com). And perhaps you may see yourself reflected in some of what I say (and if you do, I encourage you that the best way to be free is to take what I say to heart, and to ask God to break *you* down too and to rebuild your life the way He wants it to be):

Oh my! Where do I even begin? Today I spent 3 hours in the field with God...I wasn't expecting to spend 3 hours out there...but God decided to heed my request to break me down, and rebuild me how he wants me to be. He broke me down indeed. And I am thankful.

He revealed to me how hypocritically I've been living. I've been living a minimally "Christian" life, thinking (or choosing to believe) that I was doing great spiritually, because my standards happened to be a little higher than the next person's...and I got into a deep rut of spiritual pride.
But it turns out that, I had and have nothing to be "proud" about! My life was so full of compromises that it breaks my heart to think about it now - and indeed, it surely broke God's heart. Many of these compromises were things I knew weren't right, but I delighted in doing nothing about them. Some of them I just never really thought about as

11

compromises until now. And still others were things that maybe nudged at my conscience or tapped at my heart, but I quickly dismissed the nudges, murmuring something about not wanting to be "legalistic"; which was a sly way for me to hold onto many things that brought me pleasure, instead of giving them up to God.

First and foremost, I compromised in my relationship with God. I put on an "I have it all together" persona without even realizing it, when I walked into church. I thought I was close to God because I sang some songs and heard a sermon. (And I can't say that nothing came of that, because it did, but only because <u>God</u> is faithful.) Then I hung out with friends, played some games, watched some movies, talked some, and went home. Each day during the week would be a real battle against spending time with God. Often it would be with the excuse that I had other important things that needed to be done too...but now looking back, all I see is wasted day after wasted day. Sure, I spent some time reading the Bible and praying. Just enough to refill my spiritual pride tank, in case I talked to anyone who might ask. Quick enough that it didn't cut anything I wanted to do out of my day, and quick enough that I could never really tell you what happened there, because, more often than not, my heart wasn't really in it. My first and greatest desire was not spending time with God or serving Him...as much as I said it was...or read books that said it should be. There was a disconnect between what I knew and what I acted on...and I did realize that a bit...I just didn't do anything about it. I didn't even know where to start.

However, if what I have just written had been written by someone else, and I had read it a month ago - even a couple of weeks ago - I expect I would have read it, and I would have thought, "Aw, that's nice. I'm glad God woke her up. I'm glad my relationship with God is strong enough that I don't struggle with that stuff." And then I would have moved on, doing the same old thing, the same old way. Sometimes God just has to get you out of your comfort zone to <u>really</u> wake you up.

One thing that God really opened my eyes to today was that, so often I have asked God to forgive me for things simply because I felt bad, and wanted a clear conscience. But many of those times, I never said 2 little words - "I'm sorry", because my pride had me convinced that I was a-ok with God, and He wasn't bothered with how I was living my life. I wasn't truly sorry for what I had done.

So in all of this breaking me down...God also pointed out to me that I have not preserved my purity. Now this might seem strange to anyone who knows me...but keep in mind that I had been un-touched by the immense weight of God's glory in a meaningful way for so long, that my heart was growing numb. I surely haven't done anything out-rightly immoral - I don't even have a boyfriend. But I have certainly let my heart slip.

It started with watching a few "maybe they've gone too far" scenes in movies, and acting like it didn't affect me (I didn't want to be "legalistic", of course), and reading some "innocent" romancy books that maybe took their descriptions a little too far. Then it was like I was fanning into flame some embers - embers that God had given me to save for when he brings me to the guy he has been preparing me for...embers that <u>he's</u> supposed to fan...not <u>me</u>. But I did. I fanned away. And I will confess now that, though the Holy Spirit whispered "Don't," I pushed him aside, and more times than I want to *think of, indulged my flesh by watching things in secret, that I wish I had not...and I pray that I never would again. I found more pleasure in those things, than in my times with God. And the more I did that, and allowed those things to slip into my thoughts, the more I was willing to compromise in "real life" as well; and I'm sure my parents noticed...especially my mom; she's rather intuitive like that (and she talks to Jesus a lot), but I hid behind my "good girl" persona, because it was convenient, while all the time, I was willing to be less careful in what I did and said. And even though I feel like God has given me the desire to be a wife and mother, I was slowly but surely moving further and further away from that Proverbs 31 woman; a woman who will be able to serve and bless her husband, and multiply his impact, and cover him in prayer, and serve God alongside him (the woman I WANT to be), <u>despite</u> all the books I was reading about preparing for that and trusting God etc. **You can read as many books as you want, but until God is the Love of your life, and until the Bible effects every part of who you are...reading a book does nothing. It will never do anything until you let it change the way you live.**

I have also compromised in my conversation; SO often I could have encouraged someone and didn't. SO often I have been content talking about fads and empty things instead of my Savior.

And I have compromised in my witness; basically in the last few years I have become completely inward focused and selfish...and I don't think I've talked about Jesus with a single person who wasn't already a Christian. But it was "ok", because I was supposedly growing closer to God...and "preparing" for that day when someone happens across my path. But if I truly had the entire truth of the gospel in view, I would have made sure I was telling as many people as possible about Christ, and having Charles Spurgeon's view that he prayed none would go to hell un-prayed for and unwarned, and if they must go, that it would be with our arms around their ankles, pleading with them to see the truth and turn back. Without realizing it, I had succumbed to the "typical" American mindset of avoiding any kind of "conflict", and having a "me first" mentality.

Last (for now), but not least, I was so willing to compromise in the areas of movies and music. I slowly let my ipod collect more and more songs that didn't necessarily have "bad" lyrics, but they didn't draw me closer to Christ either. In fact, if anything, they only encouraged my fleshly desires, and fanciful notions of what it would be like if I had a boyfriend to spend time with...leaving God out of the picture, of course.

(*Any good desire can become an idol when we make it more important than God.*) *And as far as movies go…well, it wasn't necessarily the content that was my main problem (although I've certainly allowed more into my eyes through that medium than I should have – particularly violence and immorality), but when I spend gobs of time watching a TV show online, that doesn't seem like a wise use of time. And when I consider giving up movies for a year, but hesitate severely, because I can't* <u>stand</u> *not knowing what happens in Season 6 of this particular show for that long…or "What if God calls me to give up movies for the rest of my life?" Can I stand not knowing what happens next in the show* <u>forever</u>*? When those thoughts come up, it's clear that this is more of an idol than I had previously thought.*

All of these things - these compromises - that I've allowed into my life, I share with you, not because it's a fun pastime…not because I have nothing else to do (ha!)…not because I get some sick sense of delight in airing all of that out there (though there is really a sense of freedom in doing it)…BUT because Jesus Christ has truly set me free of the power of sin and death and I want you to know this glorious liberty as well! He has opened my eyes to all these things which I literally didn't care about or realize were sucking the life out of our relationship. And I know that He can and will do the same for each and every one of you, if you are willing to see, with the vision He gives you, the incredible desperation of your own situation, and the overwhelming grace of God when you simply, humbly, truly, at last, just say "I'm sorry", and turn from those things which have so delighted you, and find your delight in the Lord. I have honestly never felt more alive than I've felt today, and this past week. Praise the Lord for awakening my heart!

I literally feel like I never truly understood the full weight of my sin, and Christ's sacrifice and love and grace until now. I tried to "feel" something. I tried reading books about the gospel and how amazing it is. But the spiritual pride I had certainly clouded my vision…and all I saw were words, and all I heard was the same phrases…and I tried to make them mesh into my life, but that disconnect kept pushing it away.

I wanted to share this with you so that, if you have been struggling with anything like these things I mentioned, compromising in your relationship with God, you can understand that God is more than able and willing to forgive us and set us free, if we come before Him broken.

I don't want to "just survive" in this life - I want to live for Christ and serve Him with all I am. Whether it means dying for Him or living until I'm 90 for Him. Whether it means staying in North America, or going elsewhere. Whether it means having absolutely nothing other than what God provides, or a well-paying job that allows me to do things for others that way. He never said it would be easy, but He promised to always be with us. I'm ready. Are you?

I want to be like Simon and Andrew, who <u>immediately</u> left their nets at the call of Jesus. They left their own plans, and God gave them a much more wonderful purpose.

It may also be helpful for you to know that in this season of my life, I was still actively seeking the Lord. There were periods of time where I would be spending 2 or 3 hours reading my Bible and praying every day. But you know what happened? I was still watching movies – sometimes I would watch them every-other day – and listening to my worldly music (think of Taylor Swift, Colbie Callait, etc – which weren't filled with swearing or outright immorality, but which still were taking my mind off the Lord *and* filling it with other things, like relationships), and spending gobs of time online…and even though I was spending several hours a day with the Lord, I was confused as to why I wasn't really growing in the Lord like I wanted to be, or learning things from the Lord like I wanted to. It wasn't the Bible verses that stuck in my head, but movies scenes or song lyrics without any real meaning. It was like any time I filled my mind with these other things, I completely un-did all the effort I had spent seeking the Lord. It was like it had never happened. This is why being able to surrender these things to the Lord is so important. If we make an effort to begin seeking the Lord – even spending a *lot* of time with Him, and yet, we insist on holding onto our entertainment that is filling our hearts with corruption, it is like getting ourselves a big glass of fresh, cool water…and then putting just a drop or two of water from the sewer in it. Would you like to take a sip? I didn't think so. In the same way, even if we spend time with the Lord each day, our

15

entertainment and pastimes which are full of worldliness and sinfulness pollute our lives, and undo all the progress we have made.

Put This To Action:

- Spend an hour with the Lord and ask Him to show you areas in your life where you have compromised and sinned. Don't stop waiting on Him until you get answers (even if it takes longer than an hour). Bring this book or a notebook with you and write them down as God shows them to you , like I did.

_____

_____

_____

_____

_____

_____

_____

_____

_____

_____

_____

_____

_____

_____

- What is the standard by which you have been measuring yourself? Have you been comparing yourself with others, or with God's standards? Do some Bible studying on what God's standards are. Start in Exodus 20, and then read Matthew chapters 5 through 7. Then ask God to show you anywhere else you should read.
- Make a goal to have a conversation with one person about the Lord this week, and what He has been showing you and teaching you. It can be in person, or online, or through a phone call, etc.

Letter 2:

Pray Without...WHAT?!

Dear Every-girl,

1 Thessalonians 5:16-19 says, *"Rejoice always, <u>pray without ceasing</u>, in everything give thanks, for this is God's will for you in Christ Jesus. Do not quench the Spirit."*

An important part of your relationship with the Lord blossoming in beauty and depth is *actually* spending time with Him…not just Sundays, but *every* day. Sometimes we don't take our relationship with the Lord very seriously, I fear. And this may be because we don't truly love Him like we say we do, because if we really loved Him, we would spend as much time with Him as possible, because we would understand His beauty and His wisdom and *His* love for *us*, and would long to spend more time with Him and to be near Him all the time.

Many people don't seem to truly understand the sweetness that can be found in prayer. They look at it more as a duty and obligation than a privilege and blessing. Many people have their "list" when they come to pray of all the things they need to remember to ask God for, rather than just enjoying being with the Lord, and asking Him to direct their prayers.

Not that having a list of prayer needs isn't good – they can be very helpful to remember the many prayer requests you may end up with (both your own and other people's) – however, only running through your list every day and not seeking to really enter into the Lord's presence takes away the sweetest part of the relationship, just as only going through a list of everything you need when you talk to a close friend would make the friendship fizzle out. What do you do when you spend time with a friend that causes your hearts to be knit together? You talk with them about all of your dreams and hopes and fears, you listen to all of their stories too, you spend time doing fun things together – and you even spend the hard times together, if you are true friends – and you just want to hang out as often as possible. It's the same way with God – He just wants to spend time with you, to hear your heart, and to share His own.

Did you know that you can invite the Lord to be with you all throughout the day? Whatever you're doing, you can enjoy the sweetness of His company. I've been coming to understand that the Lord doesn't just barge in and *force* you to be with Him. No, He likes to be asked. And you can ask Him to come and be with you when you're going to the store, when you're making dinner, when you're playing a game – whatever you're doing! And when you ask Him, He is delighted to satisfy your request…and having His company makes everything sweeter; every gathering is more joyful, and every chore becomes a blessing. It is a special thing to be able to dwell in the presence of God *all* the time. And the more you do it, the easier it gets to remember to invite Him to be with you.

However, the Lord can't join you when you are filling your time and heart with things that are repulsive to Him...which is why what I said in the first letter is so important. And I believe that this is one reason that so many people don't spend more time with the Lord - because they *enjoy* doing things that are displeasing to the Lord, and which break His heart, and they know that if they wanted to spend more time with the Lord, and to actually be able to enter His presence, they would have to give up doing these things. The Lord would request it of them, because they cannot enter into His throne room, which is full of purity and holiness, while they are still clinging to the dirty, disgusting things of the world. And when we choose to hold onto these things instead of being willing to lay them aside or throw them out in order to be with the Lord, we are actually saying that we love our violent, sinful movies, and our novels, and our music that causes our sinful desires to grow, and wasting time on our computers, etc., MORE than we love being in the purity and brightness of the presence of the Creator of the universe, Who spoke galaxies into being, Who is full of infinite wisdom and grace, Who created every particle of everything we see, Who gave us our very lives. We would rather spend time rolling in the sewage of the world than sitting in the lap of Jesus, and listening to Him share His heart with us. We have been so deceived! And yet, of course the devil makes all the sinful and distracting things seem "fun" and attractive...and, indeed, they may seem so to us at first, but they will never satisfy us. They will leave us empty, and dirty, and they will suck away our lives, and leave us nothing in return. Proverbs 14:12-16 says, *"There is a way that seems right to a man, but its end is the way to death. Even in laughter the heart may ache, and the end of joy may be grief. The backslider in heart will be filled with the fruit of his ways, and a good man will be filled with the fruit of his ways. The simple believes everything, but the prudent gives thought to his steps. One who is wise is cautious and turns away from evil, but a fool is reckless and careless."* This is so true, and there are many people in the world who *appear* to be having fun, and who have, it seems, everything they could possibly want...but these same people are so empty because they are chasing after the devil's bait, which never has any rewards. If we are wise, we will be able to see what is evil and worthless, and turn away from it.

The only thing which can truly satisfy us is spending time with the Lord. And He created it that way because He knew it would be the best thing for us. The devil knows that, when we spend time in the Lord's presence, it is a dangerous thing, for we will be changed when the Lord fills us and when we allow Him to begin working in and through us. And the devil also knows that, when we pray for others, the strongholds he has worked so hard to construct around the people we are praying for will come crashing down as the Lord hears our prayers and begins answering them…and that is not an idea that he is very fond of. So what does he do? He works very hard (and sometimes he doesn't actually *have* to work very hard, because we are so easily distracted from the Lord and led astray) to cause us to think about other things, and do other things and esteem other things as far more important than they actually are, until any and all time that we *could* have spent praying has been smushed out of our day. And it's always a new battle to be with the Lord every day, because the devil always has hope of succeeding…and often does, with those who do not stand firm and determine to seek the Lord no matter what.

It's also essential to remember that praying for other people is very important, and when you are able to really enter into the Lord's presence and bring other people before Him, you will actually be able to see amazing answers to your prayers. And all it takes is one person earnestly pleading before the Lord on another person's behalf. One example is found in Exodus 32:9-14, *"And the LORD said to Moses, 'I have seen this people, and behold, it is a stiff-necked people. Now therefore let me alone, that my wrath may burn hot against them and I may consume them, in order that I may make a great nation of you.' But Moses implored the LORD his God and said, 'O LORD, why does your wrath burn hot against your people, whom you have brought out of the land of Egypt with great power and with a mighty hand? Why should the Egyptians say, "With evil intent did he bring them out, to kill them in the mountains and to consume them from the face of the earth"? Turn from your burning anger and relent from this disaster against your people. Remember Abraham, Isaac, and Israel, your servants, to whom you swore by your own self, and said to them, "I will multiply your offspring as the stars of heaven, and all this land that I have promised I will give to your offspring, and they shall inherit it forever."' And the LORD relented from the disaster that he had spoken of bringing on his people."*

The Lord didn't destroy the people who had been terribly wicked, because Moses pleaded for mercy on their behalf, and the Lord heard. Of course, once again, the devil does not want to see this happen - if he is unhappy when we come to the Lord just to praise Him and pray for the help *we* need, how much more is he furious when our prayers are directed at the rescue and strengthening of others as well?! However, once again, it is so very much worth it, as we don't give up, and press on in prayer, and begin to see God answering our prayers for our friends and family and co-workers and even our "enemies"!

The Holy Spirit

So what can you do when all the things I mentioned throughout this chapter come about to entice you away from the Lord and spending time with Him? What can you do when it just seems like you can't "make it" with your own strength, and everything within you just wants to give in? What do you do when you sit down to pray and you begin to feel uncomfortable and itchy and tired and every part of you is screaming to get up and do something else? God has prepared for you a beautiful and miraculous gift! His Holy Spirit is offered to you freely for the asking, to strengthen you to stand firm in the Lord – which you can't do in your own power – and to help you in all things relating to godliness. John 14:26 says, *"But the Helper, the Holy Spirit, whom the Father will send in my name, he will teach you all things and bring to your remembrance all that I have said to you."*

How do you receive this gift? All it requires is going before the Lord humbly in prayer, and asking Him to pour out His Holy Spirit into you, so that you can serve God more effectively, and resist the devil's temptations. Whenever you're struggling, you can ask for the Spirit's strengthening. When you want to talk to someone about the Lord, but you don't think you can say the right things, just ask the Holy Spirit to fill your mouth with His words for that person, and to bring to your remembrance just the right scriptures at the right time. When you are longing to understand the Bible better and to learn what God wants you to learn from what you read or hear, you can ask the Holy Spirit to teach you from it, and to show you God's heart behind the words. When you are struggling with a sin that you just can't seem to get rid of on your own, ask the Lord to send His Holy Spirit to strengthen you, and to change your heart, and to enable you to flee from the sin that has you in an iron grip. And you know what? He *will* do all these things, if we will just humble ourselves and ask for His help! That's what He is there for! Isn't that so gracious of the Lord? He doesn't expect us to be able to do it on our own…and He knows that we *can't* do it on our own – we're just usually the last ones to figure that out – but when we do, God has made a provision for us, to help us!

The Holy Spirit has also been given to you so that your life may become fruitful! A life that does not bear good fruit (which means either we may be bearing *bad* fruit, or just not bearing *any* fruit at all – which is the situation that is becoming more and more common among us as Christians, it seems) is one that is not truly living for the Lord. John 15:1-11 says, *"I am the true vine, and my Father is the vinedresser. Every branch in me that does not bear fruit he takes away, and every branch that does bear fruit he prunes, that it may bear more fruit….As the branch cannot bear fruit by itself, unless it abides in the vine, neither can you, unless you abide in me. I am the vine; you are the branches. Whoever abides in me and I in him, he it is that bears much fruit, for apart from me you can do nothing. If anyone does not abide in me he is thrown away like a branch and withers; and the branches are gathered, thrown into the fire, and burned. If you abide in me, and my words abide in you, ask whatever you wish, and it will be done for you. By this my Father is glorified, that you bear much fruit and so prove to be my disciples."* And Acts 1:8 says, *"But you will receive*

25

power when the Holy Spirit has come upon you, and you will be my witnesses in Jerusalem and in all Judea and Samaria, and to the end of the earth." If our lives are not bearing good fruit, then it's a warning sign that we are not really attached to "the Vine"…or, in other words, we are not spending the time we need to be spending with Jesus, in order that we may be filled up with His love for others, and pouring out His love into their lives.

What does it mean to be "bearing much fruit"? Well, I will go a little more into detail in another letter, but the short answer is that bearing much fruit means *doing all that we can* – big or small – for the purpose of sharing the gospel with people, and encouraging their walk with the Lord…and all this out of love for God and with His love for the people. We can't help anyone else if we aren't being taught by the Lord ourselves, and spending all the time with Him that we can. And the Holy Spirit can help you to "bear much fruit" in ways that you would never have thought of, and with a boldness and power that is not your own.

But, as the end of the first verse I shared in this letter said, we must be careful to "not quench (or extinguish) the Spirit". From what I have experienced, it seems that one way we can so easily suppress the Spirit of God is as soon as we willingly do things that go against God's purity and holiness. And, most of the time, we can't understand what's wrong with something the Lord asks us to give up or points out as wrong until we are un-tangled from its grip, and have turned away from it in order to seek the Lord. It is only then that we can start to see the filthiness and the worthlessness of the things of the world, and you begin to realize the all-surpassing worth and beauty of living each day in the Lord's presence and with the Lord's blessing and power and strength.

And another way that we can quench the Spirit's work is also simply not having faith; not believing that He is real, not believing that He will help, and not trusting that He can do great and awesome things. But a really neat thing is that, even when you are struggling to have faith in the Holy Spirit's work, you can ask Him to help you have faith, and He so graciously does!

The Holy Spirit will help us to pray the Lord's heart, as well as helping us to resist the devil's distractions and temptations. If you are struggling with something, or someone you know is struggling with something, and you just don't know exactly how to pray the best for them, the Holy Spirit can give you just the right thing to pray in that moment.

So how *can* we pray victoriously, with so much fighting against us?

First, make it of first importance. Prayer is one of the very most important parts of living our lives for Jesus. Prayer is how a Christian who does great things for the Lord *does* them…because it is, *"Not by might, nor by power, but by my Spirit, says the LORD of hosts."* (Zechariah 4:5) We must all come to the realization sooner or later that we actually cannot do anything worthwhile in our own strength, and that every battle is actually won on our knees, and that all work – even good things done for the Lord – can only be accomplished with effectiveness by much prayer…because God is the One who has the power…and we distinctly do not. But when we ask Him for His strength, and for Him to do things through situations that might look impossible, He hears and answers our prayers.

Second, don't give in. Don't give in to the feeling that you should be doing something else. Don't give in to the thought that maybe you'll just take a break from praying for a minute, and then get back into it. Don't give in to the feelings of tiredness that suddenly seem to wash over you, and think that, "Maybe I shouldn't pray right now because I'm so tired…I'll pray later…or wait for some time when my mind is more clear." If you give in now, that's a defeat on your side, and a win on the devil's side. (And if you give up, not only is it telling to the devil that he might get you to not ever pray if he continues to bring those sort of thoughts to mind, but you will likely never actually end up making the time to pray if you put it off until another time.) Press on. Press in to be with the Lord in His presence, where all those distractions and unpleasant feelings will fade away. It takes work and perseverance and determination, because actually being in God's presence is such a sweet and valuable gift, that He has made it take some work to get there, so that only those who truly want Him will find Him. But I can tell you that your perseverance will be well rewarded…for there is no peace and joy comparable to the times I am able to press past my own feelings and distracting thoughts into the presence of God and spend time with Him.

Third, pray out loud. Find somewhere you can go and pray out loud and just start talking to God like you would with your best friend. It helps a lot. When you are praying "in your head/heart" it often results in lost ends of prayers and confused or distracted thoughts. Praying out loud not only helps to keep your thoughts in order, but it makes talking with God much more personal and sweet (and effective).

Fourth, coming to the Lord with the right heart attitudes is also important for effective prayer. Being angry at God, or blaming God for things, or coming to Him with selfish requests, or having a prideful attitude are all things that will cause your prayer times not to be very effective. If you suspect any wrong motives or attitudes in your heart, you can come to God at the beginning of your time with Him and confess these things to Him, asking Him to remove those wrong attitudes from your heart and mind, and asking for His help to pray in a way that is humble and a blessing to Him. Asking God to grow in us a humble heart is always a good place to start, so that we can come to Him in prayer with our minds thinking on His goodness and power and faithfulness, etc....and not on our own selfishness or prideful anger, or whatever it may be that is wrong in our hearts. We must keep at the forefront of our minds that God is always good, and never does anything from a wrong motive, and He never makes a mistake...and He also has no obligation to answer our prayers the way we think He should...but He will answer...and His answer will always be for good.

Also, try praying more specific prayers. For example, instead of praying for grandma to have a good day, pray that God would relieve the pain of her arthritis, that she would feel God's presence beside her all day, or that God would give her a specific encouragement from scripture that day that's exactly what she needs (or any number of things that God might lead you to pray, if you ask Him). Praying specific things for specific people gives you something to look back at and praise the Lord for when He answers your specific prayers. These answers are especially useful to cling to when you are tempted to doubt that God is really listening. As I've begun making more specific requests of the Lord, it seems that He is more than glad to answer them , to show His power over each situation and His care for each person. And it's so much more amazing when you've been praying for something in specific, and God answers your prayer - a thrill of joy and praise to God just fills your heart! God just loves to grow our faith. Chances are that if you simply pray general prayers for people to have a good day or for things to go well, you won't get the same excitement when God answers, because you didn't really take the time to think over what you were praying about, which *may* also mean that you didn't really have the full confidence that God would answer a more specific prayer, so without really realizing it, you tried to make it "easier" for him. This isn't true faith! And God doesn't need us to make our prayers "easier" for Him to answer. God loves to answer big prayers, which show that we truly believe that He is BIG and has power over all things. If anything, He would love for us to be asking greater things of Him, and trusting that He is good, and that He loves to answer His children when they pray with all of their heart.

And what about those times when you don't feel like God is listening or answering? Repeat God's truths out loud…and spend time just praising the Lord, and singing songs about His goodness, and thanking Him for all the wonderful things that you know He *has* done. Some good scriptures to remember are:

"And he told them a parable to the effect that they ought always to pray and not lose heart. He said, 'In a certain city there was a judge who neither feared God nor respected man. And there was a widow in that city who kept coming to him and saying, "Give me justice against my adversary." For a while he refused, but afterward he said to himself, "Though I neither fear God nor respect man, yet because this widow keeps bothering me, I will give her justice, so that she will not beat me down by her continual coming."' And the Lord said, 'Hear what the unrighteous judge says. And will not God give justice to his elect, who cry to him day and night? Will he delay long over them? I tell you, he will give justice to them speedily. Nevertheless, when the Son of Man comes, will he find faith on earth?'" Luke 18:1-8 - This is an awesome parable to remember, told by Jesus Himself (and He knows *all* about prayer and how it works), for our encouragement that God rewards persistent prayer; He rewards the prayer of His children who do not give up and are not easily discouraged from praying; those who persist until they get an answer (and this is displayed many times throughout the Bible).

"'Ask, and it will be given to you; seek, and you will find; knock, and it will be opened to you. For everyone who asks receives, and the one who seeks finds, and to the one who knocks it will be opened. Or which one of you, if his son asks him for bread, will give him a stone? Or if he asks for a fish, will give him a serpent? If you then, who are evil, know how to give good gifts to your children, how much more will your Father who is in heaven give good things to those who ask him!'" Matthew 7:7-11 – These words of Jesus give us confidence that, when we pray, we should come with faith that God is good and

kind, and that His answers to our prayers will be with equal goodness and kindness.

"Let us then with confidence draw near to the throne of grace, that we may receive mercy and find grace to help in time of need." Hebrews 4:16

Put This To Action:

- Ask yourself if you <u>really</u> love the Lord, or are you trying to spend as little time as possible with Him so it doesn't interrupt the things you want to do?
- Take a walk today outside, and begin talking out loud to the Lord, and just enjoying spending time with Him. (If you aren't able to go outside to talk aloud to Him, then try to find a place in your home that you can use as a 'prayer closet,' where you can pray aloud uninterrupted.)
- Make it a goal today to invite the Lord to be with you whenever you begin doing something new. Tell Him you just want to spend time with Him, and you want to have the sweetness of His company, and even His help with whatever you're working on. Do the same thing again tomorrow.
- Before you do the things you normally do, ask yourself if Jesus would be comfortable being with you as you do it. If not, it probably isn't worth doing, and you may be able to find a much better use for your time. (Example: instead of watching a worldly TV show, try reading your Bible, praying, writing a letter, etc.)
- Consider asking the Holy Spirit to come and fill you to help you resist the temptations of the devil and to strengthen you to serve the Lord better. Receiving the baptism of the Holy Spirit is such an amazing gift from the Lord…and it is so powerful that it transformed bumbling and doubting disciples of Jesus into men who were on fire for Him, and only wanted to tell others about Him, and were even willing to die for Him.
- Put your prayer time as the first thing on your schedule each day of this week so you can practice putting prayer first…and start trying the different principles of prayer found in this chapter.
- List 3 people that you are going to begin praying for (at least one of them should be unsaved, unless you don't know anyone who is unsaved):

———————————————————————————————

———————————————————————————————

———————————————————————————————

Letter 3:

The Bible – God's Very Words!

Dear Every-girl,

"So Jesus said…. 'If you abide in my word, you are truly my disciples, and you will know the truth, and the truth will set you free.'" John 8:31-32

Proverbs 9:10 says, *"The fear of the LORD is the beginning of wisdom, and the knowledge of the Holy One is insight."* What is the "fear of the Lord"? Fearing the Lord does not mean that we should literally be afraid of Him. Proverbs 8:13 says, *"The fear of the LORD is hatred of evil. Pride and arrogance and the way of evil and perverted speech I hate."*

More on the fear of the Lord in Proverbs:

* It is the beginning of **knowledge**. (Proverbs 1:7)
* It is <u>hatred of evil</u>. (Proverbs 8:15)
* It is the beginning of **wisdom** and insight. (Proverbs 9:10)
* It <u>prolongs life</u>. (Proverbs 10:27)
* It gives strong **confidence**. (Proverbs 14:26)
* It is a fountain of **life.** (Proverbs 14:27)
*It is instruction in wisdom. (Proverbs 15:33)
* It is **strength** to turn away from evil. (Proverbs 16:6)
* It <u>leads to life</u> and **satisfies**. (Proverbs 19:23)
* Its reward= riches and honor and life. (Proverbs 22:4)

A quote from the ESV Study Bible notes says it very well, "Any society that commonly assumes that God will not discipline sin in this life or judge it in the next will have no fear of God and will therefore give itself increasingly to evil."

So "the fear of the Lord" means that we should have a humble, worshipful view of God and a right understanding of His character (which is holy and pure and righteous), His commands, and His power. All of these things will lead our hearts to rightly fearing Him – having a healthy fear of His displeasure and discipline – and to understanding the disgustingness of sin and evil in God's sight, and it will cause our hearts to long to be clean for Him. If we fear the Lord, we are on the way to having true wisdom! As you saw in Proverbs 9:10, it said, "the knowledge of the Holy One is insight", and as I said, fear of the Lord comes from really *knowing* Him and understanding His character. And where do we get this knowledge from? We get it from spending time with the Lord Himself, and reading His Word! God's words are full of wisdom which leads to salvation, and is profitable and important for those desiring to live a godly life. (2 Tim. 3:14-17)

Let me just be clear about something before we go any further. It is a very common lie that the devil likes to try to make all of us believe at some point in our lives *that the Bible is boring.* Let me assure you that the Bible is *not* "boring"! It is actually one of the most intriguing and exciting books ever written…and most wonderful of all, reading it will change your life. The devil is pretty clever, and has actually kept many people from reading the Bible with that lie....but by God's grace, he will no longer be able to keep *you* from reading the Bible because of it.

Just imagine the King of the entire Universe – of galaxies un-numbered, of planets and stars and moons (all different and unique), of our own planet, of the waterfalls and the mountains which reach into the sky, of the brilliantly colored fish which swim in turquoise waters, of each tree and each blade of grass...and *us*- humans with complexities which reach far deeper than even just the physical things (though the physical things are still quite complicated themselves). Imagine that the King and Creator of all this wrote *you* a letter, explaining how you could get to know Him, and telling you all about things He's created and what He's done for people...and how He wants to do these same things for you! Wouldn't you want to read that letter?

Well, you can! This is exactly what we have when we hold the Bible in our hands. The Bible is God's very own words, carefully chosen to share His heart with us, which He has kept watch over for ages, so that it would be able to speak to us today just as clearly as when He spoke to Moses on Mount Sinai. And His words are more alive today, a few thousand years later, than the words of any other book you could ever read, because, like I mentioned in the last letter, God has given His Holy Spirit to teach us as we read them, and because there is eternal truth in every single one of them. Hebrews 4:12 says, *"For the word of God is living and active, sharper than any two-edged sword, piercing to the division of soul and of spirit, of joints and of marrow, and discerning the thoughts and intentions of the heart."* Which leads me to the next point I would like to make, which is:

God's words (the Bible) are a powerful weapon of defense against the devil and all his lies and schemes, and they are also a weapon for the use of winning souls for the Kingdom of God! Ephesians 6 says, *"Finally, be strong in the Lord and in the strength of his might. Put on the whole armor of God, that you may be able to stand against the schemes of the devil.....Stand therefore, having fastened on the belt of truth, and having put on the breastplate of righteousness, and, as shoes for your feet, having put on the readiness given by the gospel of peace. In **all circumstances** take up the shield of faith, with which you can extinguish all the flaming darts of the evil one; and take the helmet of salvation, and **the sword of the Spirit, which is the word of God**, praying at all* *times in the Spirit, with all prayer and supplication. To that end keep alert with all perseverance, making supplication for all the saints…"*

When we <u>read</u> and <u>study</u> and <u>memorize</u> scripture, God can bring it to our minds at just the right times. He can bring it to our minds in order to destroy the lies of the devil as he tries to cause us to doubt God or to be filled with fear or as he tries to tell us that it's not worth it to serve the Lord…any number of things.

God can also bring scriptures to our minds in a conversation with a Christian friend who is struggling…and when God brings just the right scripture to mind, it can actually minister to their hearts in a very deep way, unlike our own words, which can never truly help them in the ways they really need like the Bible can *("Let the word of Christ dwell in you richly, teaching and admonishing one another in all wisdom, singing psalms and hymns and spiritual songs, with thankfulness in your hearts to God."* Colossians 3:16).

God can also bring scriptures to mind as we talk with someone who is not a Christian, as they may have strong arguments against Christianity that we could never argue with or diffuse in our own reasoning…but even the strongest argument can be undone with just one scripture which states things in such a clear, firm, and undeniable way that it can quickly leave the scoffers speechless…and even cause them to realize that they were wrong. *"Walk in wisdom toward outsiders, making the best use of the time. Let your speech always be gracious, seasoned with salt, so that you may know how you ought to answer each person."* Colossians 4:5-6

Scripture can also help us to know when something is not true or Biblical (saving us from following after empty or even harmful teachings), even in the case of prophets – for there are people who call themselves "prophets", but they do not speak God's words, and many people are captivated by what they say because it sounds pleasing, but it goes against God's Word. As Jeremiah 23:26-29 says, *"How long shall there be lies in the heart of the prophets who prophesy lies, and who prophesy the deceit of their own heart, who think to make my people forget my name by their dreams that they tell one another, even as their fathers forgot my name for Baal? Let the prophet who has a dream tell the dream, **but let him who has my word speak my word faithfully**. What has straw in common with wheat? declares the LORD. **Is not my word like fire, declares the LORD, and like a hammer that breaks the rock in pieces?**"* God's Word completely destroys even the hardest lies, and brings a complete end to them. And dreams and prophecies have nothing in comparison with God's own words, and we should always evaluate and test what we hear based on scripture first and foremost. If it does not agree with the Bible and with God's character, then it's not worth listening to. And if you're wondering about a dream or something you've seen yourself…just remember that not all dreams are from the Lord: the devil can speak quite loudly, and sometimes we are tempted to believe what he says because it sounds *good*…but God's is the still small voice. And whatever He says is for our spiritual growth, to draw us closer to Him. Even if you are convinced some prophecy or dream was from the Lord, don't follow it or look to it for guidance more than you look to the Bible. Always run to the Bible first when you are looking for guidance and help in any situation. It is just as helpful and true today as it ever was. And if you are truly seeking after the Lord, He will direct your steps whether or not you understand where He is leading you. (A side note: Be very careful of prophetic meetings today, because many who call themselves prophets have actually turned the real and godly gift into a money-making venture which ends up being more like fortune-telling than speaking the words of God. Ask God to give you His discernment of what is true and what is false in these situations. And it is of great importance for you to read your Bible. Many "false prophets" and teachers will quote half of a verse, or take a verse completely out of context in order to make their teaching sound true and Biblical, but you will never be able to tell what is true or what is false if you don't study God's Word.)

Another important thing we must realize is that we *need to be "doers" of God's words – not just hearers.* And we can't *do* what we haven't read. And the thing is that, if we read the Bible and then get up and walk away from it, having forgotten what we read, it's just the same as if we'd never read it. The Bible and what it says shouldn't be taken lightly. It is alive and full of eternal truth…and it's a matter of life and death. Once we have read something from the Bible, we are responsible for the knowledge we now have, and we are responsible for what we do (or don't do) with it. God sees everything.

Let me tell you that there is quite a difference between simply reading the Bible and actually studying the Bible and desiring to learn what God would want to teach you from it. I was one of those people who, for a long while, would simply read a chapter of the Bible as fast as I could just so I could say I had done it…instead of having a teachable heart, and realizing the great treasures which could be found within the pages of the Bible. That is not the way to grow in the Lord and in wisdom. It is also not wise to make the only Bible reading you do simply opening your Bible at random and pointing to a verse, and expecting that to be God's words for you that day, and that's all. I don't doubt that God has used this method before to confirm things to His people, but this should not be your normal practice and should certainly not be a replacement for reading God's Word – the whole thing. When we are studying the Bible we also need to remember to read things in context. Many people will take verses out of context (meaning, they read only one verse, without reading before and after it for several verses or chapters, to see how it fits into the whole story), and they will end up with conclusions based on only one verse, which are against God's heart and what He really meant, all because they did not take the time to read the rest of the book, and did not take enough time in the Lord's presence to really understand His heart and character. When you really understand the character of the Lord, it makes it much easier to tell when something is not true.

Imagine a king of a large country, full of wealth and beauty inviting *you* into his chambers- into his very own home. He invites you in with the full knowledge that all his treasures are lining his halls, and filling every free corner of his home, and not minding at all that you'll see it. And, in fact, he even invites you in actually *meaning* for you to be able to look at these treasures *and* touch them *and* hold them *and* even use them, if you want to!

No king or president just does that; none of them would invite just a normal person like you or I into their private homes…and they certainly wouldn't want us touching their most valuable things. But you know what? This is exactly what Jesus has done! Song of Solomon 1:4 says, *"Draw me after you; let us run. The King has brought me into his chambers."* God invites us into His personal chambers – even His treasure chambers, and He lets us experience all the treasures He has within for as long as we are willing to stay! If we look at reading God's Word without any real desire, it's like giving up the opportunity to see all the treasures of the greatest King who ever lived. And yet, even more than that, it's giving up the treasure of eternal life with Jesus. And you should ponder that with some measure of fear.

Another lie that we commonly believe is that *the Bible is too hard to understand.* And the truth is, of course…it's not. God has made His Word to be clear and easy to understand for even the worst of scholars. It is for those from the poorest to the rich, and from the unschooled to those who have been through their doctorate degree. When Jesus first came to earth, He was speaking to a bunch of unschooled shepherds and tradesmen and fishermen…and they understood His words better than the Pharisees and all those who *had* an education. You may have a little difficulty understanding some parts; we all do. Just pray and ask Jesus to help you understand and keep reading and praying, and He will teach you. Also, if there's a word you don't understand, just pull out a dictionary and look it up! Not only will you better understand the verse, but you'll begin to increase your vocabulary, and the whole Bible will get easier and easier to understand if you don't give up. There are also several good versions that have been translated that are much easier to understand than the King James Version (which is good, but uses words, and ways of constructing sentences that aren't in common use any more, and are sometimes hard to understand). One trustworthy version is the English Standard Version (or "ESV"), which is what I've used for this book. Another is the New American Standard Bible (or NASB). These aren't the only good choices, but they are both literal translations, and the words are taken directly from the Hebrew and Greek words in the manuscripts as they were preserved. Try to stay away from paraphrased versions, even if they seem like they might be easier to read, because many take God's words and say them in a way that wasn't exactly what God meant, and they will only confuse you and give you wrong ideas about scripture. If you decide to read a paraphrased version, just keep in mind that it is only someone's personal opinion about what the Bible means, and it should be compared with the true Bible. God can still use paraphrases, but you will be able to completely trust the straight word of God without wondering if it's true or not.

And you may wonder, "What if I don't like to read?" Well…simply owning a Bible is not going to help you have a right relationship with the Lord and to know the truth of scripture. God has put the truths in scripture which are essential to living our lives as Christians…and you can't just take what a pastor says on Sunday morning as the only time you hear the Bible. If you don't like to read, try finding an audio version of someone reading the Bible that you can listen to. But even better than that is praying that God would help you, and pressing on even if it's hard for you and just reading several verses or just one chapter a day, and asking God to teach you from it. God will reward every bit of effort you make in order to pursue Him, and to know Him better.

So where should you start? Is having 66 books in the Bible intimidating? I suggest beginning in the New Testament…and the book of Matthew is a splendid starting point, since it outlines Jesus' whole life and teachings, which by themselves can change your life.

So don't put it off until tomorrow…because the devil and the world will make sure there's never time. Do it as soon as you can. Start *now*.

Put This To Action:

- Read Proverbs 1, 2 Timothy 2, and Deuteronomy chapters 3 and 4.
- Pick 2 verses to memorize which can be used as "weapons" against the attacks of the devil (Example: If you struggle with fear, try memorizing 2 Timothy 1:7).

_____

_____

_____

_____

- Start reading 1 chapter of the Bible every day. If you aren't sure where to start, try Matthew. When you can do this consistently, try reading 2 chapters a day.
- Write down one thing you've read in the Bible recently that you want to start doing and acting on:

_____

_____

_____

_____

_____

_____

Letter 4:

Storms

Dear Every-girl,

  "Count it all joy, my brothers, <u>when</u> you meet trials of various kinds, for you know that the testing of your faith produces steadfastness. And let steadfastness have its full effect, that you may be perfect and complete, lacking in nothing." James 1:2-4

  "Blessed is the man <u>who remains steadfast</u> under trial, for when he has stood the test he will receive the crown of life, which God has promised to those who love him." James 1:12

  "Beloved, <u>do not be surprised</u> at the fiery trial when it comes upon you to test you, as though something strange were happening to you. <u>But rejoice</u> insofar as you share Christ's sufferings, that you may also rejoice and be glad when his glory is revealed. If you are insulted for the name of Christ, you are blessed, because the Spirit of glory and of God rests upon you. But let none of you suffer as a murderer or a thief or an evildoer or as a meddler. Yet if anyone suffers as a Christian, let him not be ashamed, but let him glorify God in that name....Therefore let those who suffer according to God's will entrust their souls to a faithful Creator while doing good." 1 Peter 4:12-19

  At this point you may be a little nervous about reading the rest of this letter. Why did I use all of those verses about trials? Well, there's a very good reason, actually, and if you haven't experienced it yet, you will: every one of us will go through trials and "hard times"...and being a Christian doesn't mean that you get a free card that says that you now don't have to go through anything that's hard or unpleasant. Nope. And, in fact, the Bible says the very opposite; it says that we will experience even more trials when we become Christians because the world hates the very One who has saved us, and they will now look at us with the same contempt. We should count this as a blessing! To be able to suffer for the sake of Christ is an honor, and in the end, none of the teasing, or scorn, or persecution really matters in comparison to knowing Christ. And our time on this earth full of sin is so short in comparison to eternity; this is only a small speck of time in the vastness of eternity, and this is the only time we *get* to suffer for the Lord, and to prove our love for Him, and to store up heavenly treasures.

Also, the more earnestly we are seeking the Lord, and desiring to know Him better, and serve Him more completely, the more trials we will encounter, because the devil is not happy when we run from all his enticements and distractions and begin to spend time with the Lord and begin to tell other people about Him and begin to learn that all the "treasures" of this earth are actually completely worthless in comparison with the eternal treasures that await us, and the treasure of being with the Lord.

Another reason we may experience trials is because the Lord is simply testing us and refining us, and He desires to make us more like Him…and many times we don't learn the lessons we need to unless we are put in a difficult situation. So, many trials are tools that God is using to teach us lessons, and to cause us to pray more earnestly and to seek Him more wholeheartedly.

So it doesn't sound very appealing to you? You might think to yourself that it just might not be worth it to be a Christian if you still have to go through trials your whole life. But the truth is that life without the Lord is empty and meaningless. And life *with* the Lord is filled with His joy and peace and amazing fruitfulness and purpose even in the midst of trials, when they come. On our worst days, we can have more joy than what someone who does not know the Lord has on their best day ever. *"There are many who say, 'Who will show us some good? Lift up the light of your face upon us, O LORD!' You have put more joy in my heart than they have when their grain and wine abound."* Psalm 4:6-7

The reason I needed to write this letter to you is because many young girls – and many older people too – think that, when they say the prayer to accept Jesus into their lives, everything will magically be easy and happy, because no one wants to tell them the hard things that they might encounter, because they just want people to say the prayer and to be saved. This is a noble motive…but when trials come, many people so often turn from seeking the Lord because they think their decision to become a Christian wasn't real, or didn't "work" because they are having a hard time. I don't want the storms of life to run your "ship" aground. Many people are derailed and their relationship with the Lord is wrecked because of trials and the storms of life, because their faith was not firmly rooted in the Lord, and their relationship with the Lord was not strong enough to uphold them in these times. However, every trial *will* work out for your good and growth if you trust and hold fast to Jesus.

Some important things to remember if you want to continue flourishing and growing in your relationship with the Lord even in the middle of trials are found in the verses above, and include:

- Understanding that God uses trials to refine us and make us more like Him.

- Keeping our eyes on the eternal perspective; what God sees, and understanding that everything on this earth will pass away, and only what is done for the Lord will last and will bring forth eternal joy and everlasting treasure.

- Persevering and not giving up the fight to seek the Lord and serve the Lord.

- Rejoicing in the midst of trials, that we could be counted worthy of such an honor as to suffer in the service of the Lord, without complaining.

- Praying and entrusting ourselves into the Lord's hands, and asking for His protection and defense against the devil. *"...the Lord knows how to rescue the godly from trials..."* 2 Peter 2:9a

While some trials are from the devil (and sometimes it's actually comforting to know the devil is upset...because it means that you are doing something right!), other trials are from the Lord, and for our good, to teach us things...and we should be very cautious about giving the devil more credit than he's due. I think he sometimes begins to take delight in stirring up more storms in the lives of people when he sees that he gets credit for it!

A little while ago, I was reading Matthew 14:22-33, and praying that the Lord would teach me something new from it. He did, and I believe it could be an encouragement to you as it has been to me. But first I will share the verses:

"Immediately he made the disciples get into the boat and go before him to the other side, while he dismissed the crowds. And after he had dismissed the crowds, he went up on the mountain by himself to pray. When evening came, he was there alone, but the boat by this time was a long way from the land, beaten by the waves, for the wind was against them. And in the fourth watch of the night he came to them, walking on the sea. But when the disciples saw him walking on the sea, they were terrified, and said, 'It is a ghost!' and they cried out in fear. But immediately Jesus spoke to them, saying, 'Take heart; it is I. Do not be afraid.'

And Peter answered him, 'Lord, if it is you, command me to come to you on the water.' He said, 'Come.' So Peter got out of the boat and walked on the water and came to Jesus. But when he saw the wind, he was afraid, and beginning to sink he cried out, 'Lord, save me.' Jesus immediately reached out his hand and took hold of him, saying to him, 'O you of little faith, why did you doubt?' And when they got into the boat, the wind ceased. And those in the boat worshiped him, saying, 'Truly you are the Son of God.'"

So there were the disciples, in their boat, in the middle of a violent storm which they had been battling for *hours* (the 4th watch of the night would have been between 3 and 6 am). Had the water been calm, they might have been fast asleep (or *most* of them), either still onboard the boat, or having made it to their destination and deciding to find a place to stay…and they would have missed seeing Jesus walking on the water; they would have missed seeing His power displayed in such a miraculous way! But as it was, they were awake and alert, as the wind and waves raged on the sea, and they all saw Jesus as He walked on the water toward them. They were probably pretty worn out, but it seems to me that Jesus used the storm as a means to keep them alert so that they would see His glory, and see that He is truly Lord of all creation, and by doing so, increase their faith and trust in Him.

In the same way, the Lord seems to use trials in our lives to keep us alert, so that we don't become complacent, self-satisfied, or spiritually "drowsy", and so He can come to us in the midst of them, in even the most seemingly impossible ways, and reveal to us His glory, which causes us to worship Him in truth. We cannot doubt when we see God coming towards us - the wind and the waves not even causing Him a second thought. He walks upon them with no "safety net" to fall back on, as *we* cling to the sides of our boat with white knuckles, not realizing that, if we truly trusted God, we could leave our boats, and no longer have any need to fear them being smashed to bits. We would be safer *out* of our boats and *with* Him, than if we were still in a boat; if we only had the faith to walk by Jesus' side, and not doubt that He would uphold us, and do mighty things. And we realize we have nothing at all to fear when He is near us, for the largest waves and the most blinding storms are all merely tools in His hand, with no power to crush us apart from His command…for, without a word, when all His plans for us and our growth and His glory are accomplished, the storm will cease in an instant, with no trace remaining, and the only things to remind us that it happened will be the stories of Christ's faithfulness and grace – how He came to us in the midst of it – and we will have Christ Himself in the boat beside us. Though in the midst of the storm Christ may seem distant or like a ghost and we may be tempted to think that perhaps He was just an illusion, when it is over, we will find that He is closer to us than when the storm began.

I was just reading in Psalm 11:5 that, *"The Lord tests the **righteous**, but his soul hates the wicked and the one who loves violence."*

Being in a "storm" doesn't mean that you've necessarily done something wrong, or that you should be filled with fear. On the contrary, if you are in a storm, it is likely that God is doing something wonderful. Jesus *directed* His disciples out to the sea before Him <u>so</u> He could show Himself mighty to them. If your life is going great, and you're comfortable, and everything is going your way…you may have more cause to be concerned than if you're in a trial. As Psalm 10 says, the Lord lets the wicked prosper in their earthly pursuits and earthly treasure…but the Lord chastens and tests those He loves, and refines them through the fire.

I have also recently been reading through the book of Daniel, and have been greatly encouraged by the story of Shadrach, Meshach, and Abednego being thrown into the fiery furnace because they wouldn't worship any god but the True God. (Daniel, Chapter 3.) There are several valuable lessons we can learn from it about going through trials. This is a good opportunity for you to grab your Bible and read the story – it will only take a few minutes. Go.

First of all, remember that these three men had not done anything wrong, but they had actually stood up for the Lord, and had not given in to worshipping any other god. This is the very act which got them thrown into the fire. In the same way, when we begin to stand up for the Lord, and to desire to be holy before Him, we may find ourselves thrown into trials (even the criticism or hatred of friends and family). This does not mean we've done something wrong, but that we are on the right path – the same one that Shadrach, Meshach, and Abednego walked!

I found it interesting how, in verses 22-23, the king's men were killed by the extreme heat of the fire, but God's men were completely un-touched by it and it didn't affect them in any way. When we trust that the Lord is with us in every trial, He will sustain us and fill us with joy in situations that would crush those who don't know the Lord.

From verses 24-25, I found it greatly encouraging to see that the Lord was walking with the three men in the midst of the fire. When we go through fiery trials, it is actually in these times that we often have the closest and sweetest times walking with the Lord through them.

And Charles Spurgeon (a very godly preacher from the 1800's) points out in a sermon on this passage that the 3 men lost their bonds in the furnace; a true Christian's losses are his gains. Anything that we lose going through a trial will actually set us free, and help us to be able to walk more closely with the Lord. And…they did not actually lose anything else – none of their clothes, and not a single hair. We will never lose anything that is actually worth keeping when we go through a trial.

One last thing that is neat to notice is that, after the king calls the three men out of the furnace, all of the official people of the land (the same ones who had been gathered from all over the land to worship the king's golden idol) got to see the glory of God with their own eyes (in verse 27) and to hear the king's own praise of this God. The 3 men didn't even have to say anything; everyone knew that their God had rescued them because they had been so bold about only serving <u>Him</u> beforehand. Many times, God will use trials in the lives of His children to reveal His power to those who do not yet know Him.

If by trials and storms I may be kept alert for His service, if by them I may be kept from ever becoming complacent or inward focused or full of spiritual pride again, if by them I myself – or others – may be drawn nearer to Christ, then I would welcome them, and pray that He would strengthen me to remain steadfastly fixed on Him, rejoicing through whatever comes.

By His strength may you, may I – may *we* – come forth as gold!

Put This To Action:

- Have you gone through a trial recently? Pray and ask the Lord to show you what he wants you to learn from it. Write down some of the things your trial can teach you/or what it *has* taught you:

_____

_____

_____

_____

_____

_____

_____

_____

_____

_____

_____

_____

_____

_____

_____

- When you begin struggling with a trial – big or small – start praising God for His goodness and love, and start telling Him how much you love and trust Him, instead of falling into a pity-party for yourself.
- When you are in a trial, pray often, and read your Bible to find the truth. God may be trying to get you to seek Him more earnestly through the trial.
- There are times when trials can be too heavy to bear alone. Seek out godly counsel and prayer support from older, firmly-grounded believers who have walked with God for a long time through their own trials. They will be able to be a great support to you.

Letter 5:

Parents *and* Forgiveness

Dear Every-girl,

This is going to be a fairly short, but important letter, and I'm praying that your heart will be open to the truth of what I am about to say…because it goes against the culture, and it's very likely that you have been ensnared in thinking this way.

I'm going to talk to you about your parents, because the Bible actually has a lot to say about parents, and it may be things that you haven't taken seriously before. God intended parents to be one of life's sweetest blessings, but the devil always tries to corrupt the things that God wants to bless us with the most…and the devil certainly does a good job at destroying these relationships, which could be the greatest help to us, if God was allowed to have His way.

In the 10 commandments, God says, *"Honor your father and your mother, that your days may be long in the land that the LORD your God is giving you."*(Exodus 20:12)

God doesn't give us any wiggle-room. He doesn't say we only have to honor them when they do what we want, or when they are Christians, or when they are nice to us, or only when we are little toddlers. Nope. God simply says we must honor them, with the understanding that it must be at all times, throughout all the years of our lives.

There was a time in my own life after I had graduated from high school and had my own car that God taught me this lesson. We had been going to a church that I absolutely loved for several years. I didn't really have any friends except the ones who went to this church. So, when my parents decided one day to look for another church, I was confronted with a hard decision. Because I was technically old enough to move out and get my own apartment and do what I wanted, I had to decide whether I would continue going to this church that I loved even though my parents had left, or whether I would also leave just because my parents thought it was how the Lord was leading them, even though I didn't agree with them. I went through several weeks of struggling in my heart and wrestling in prayer, and then, I knew God had spoken to me clearly. God wanted me to honor my parents' choice to leave the church, and to stay with them, even though I so badly wanted to stay where my friends all were, and to trust that He would bless my decision to honor my parents, as He has said in His word. So, my last Sunday at the church I loved was filled with lots of tears and hugs (and we lived far enough away from the church that I was pretty sure I wouldn't get to see my friends very often any more)…and it was one of the hardest things I've ever had to do, to tell my friends that I was leaving and not coming back. But I did. And though it was hard, I also felt a measure of peace, because I knew that I was obeying the Lord…even if I didn't fully understand. This was in March, I believe. Then that whole summer I followed my parents wherever they thought God was leading them without grumbling…and you know what God did? After an entire summer of being away from our church, God directed my parents to go back…and it was such a sweet thing knowing that I had done as God had asked, and He had restored the desire that I'd had to give up to obey Him, and to honor my parents.

It's not always easy to honor our parents, and in fact, it's often very hard – especially if we have gotten used to being dishonoring to them – but God will bless every step we take, and every desire we sacrifice in order to honor them, and to obey them.

"Children, obey your parents in everything, for this pleases the Lord." Colossians 3:20

The Lord also has some very serious words to say about dishonoring parents in Proverbs 30:17, which should instill some measure of fear in us, *"The eye that mocks a father and scorns to obey a mother will be picked out by the ravens of the valley and eaten by the vultures."*

And in 2 Timothy 3:1-5 and Romans, God looks at the sin of being disobedient to our parents as being just as bad as murder and hating God. And, indeed, if we disobey God's commands to respect and honor our parents, it is acting like we hate Him and His good laws.

"But understand this, that in the last days there will come times of difficulty. For people will be lovers of self, lovers of money, proud, arrogant, abusive, <u>disobedient to their parents</u>, ungrateful, unholy, heartless, unappeasable, slanderous, without self-control, brutal, not loving good, treacherous, reckless, swollen with conceit, lovers of pleasure rather than lovers of God, having the appearance of godliness, but denying its power. Avoid such people." 2 Timothy 3:1-5

"And since they did not see fit to acknowledge God, God gave them up to a debased mind to do what ought not to be done. They were filled with all manner of unrighteousness, evil, covetousness, malice. They are full of envy, murder, strife, deceit, maliciousness. They are gossips, slanderers, haters of God, insolent, haughty, boastful, inventors of evil, <u>disobedient to parents</u>, foolish, faithless, heartless, ruthless. Though they know God's righteous decree that those

who practice such things deserve to die, they not only do them but give approval to those who practice them." Romans 1:28-32

The interesting thing about these verses, which are full of so many ungodly traits, is that they are talking about people who actually call themselves Christians! This should cause us to think very seriously about these things. So, if these things are true, we need to learn how to do what the Lord expects from us.

And I bring these things up because I have known many girls who went to church and said they loved the Lord, but who were extremely disrespectful to their parents, and they thought it was ok, and even normal. And I know many girls who struggle to honor their parents as they get older, because they think they ought to be able to do what they want because they are "old enough".

It is really something that we all struggle with, because in our pride, we think we know what is best, and that we ought to be able to do what we want. But these aren't God's expectations. If we can't learn to respect our earthly parents, how can we expect to have a right relationship with our Heavenly

Father? This whole life is a training ground for us, to prepare us to be citizens of Heaven.

The best thing you can do is pray and ask the Holy Spirit to search your heart, and show you all the ways you have not honored your parents, so you can repent and ask for God's forgiveness for those things, and then ask for His help not to do them anymore. Chances are that you know when you're not treating your parents like you should, so getting started in figuring out what is wrong with your attitude and heart should be fairly easy. God is most concerned about your heart, and what is going on in it. All of your outward responses to your parents come from sinful attitudes inside your heart. Changing your attitude toward them may be difficult at first, especially if you have gotten used to being unkind toward them, or thinking of them as annoying, or being harsh with them – it may be hard at first to un-train yourself from all of these habits of thought. But ask God to help you, and to remind you, and He will. And when you make a mistake, just go to God and to your parents and apologize.

If you aren't sure where to begin, just a few of the things that are displeasing to God, but are accepted by the world, and so easy to slip into are:

- Rolling your eyes when they say something. This is very disrespectful and shows that your heart is full of pride.
- Talking badly about them to your friends. This is the same as "slander" and "gossip" which are also addressed in the Romans 1 verses above, and are things for which we deserve to die. This means sharing their faults, or mistakes, or things they did that you thought were dumb; talking about them without mercy when they aren't there. This is not pleasing to the Lord.
- Ignoring what they ask you to do, or not doing it until you feel like it.
- Saying you hate them – this is the same as murder in God's eyes.
- Arguing with them. This can be so easy to do if we aren't careful, but God wants us to be humble and to joyfully obey what is asked of us, even if we don't agree or understand. This doesn't mean you can't share your opinion in a respectful, gentle way…but if your parent doesn't agree with your opinion, it is your duty before the Lord to do as they wish, and not to argue with them.
- Being disrespectful in your replies….saying "whatever" or "I don't care" or things like these are not right.
- Doing what you want when you want to do it, without asking your parents….or doing what you want, even if they say no.

These are just a few things for you to ponder to get you started. God has given parents charge of their children, to provide for them, to instruct them, to discipline them, and to love them…and we undermine all that God has asked them to do when we don't respect them.

So what *do* you do if you parents are actually mean to you or don't care about you or aren't Christians? Well, first, God still asks us to honor them. Just because someone else is unkind or hurtful to us doesn't give us the right to do the same to them. Ask God to fill your heart with His love for them, which is unconditional – not based on anything they do or don't do. Respect them in all you do and say. Pray for them daily, and ask God to draw them to Himself, and to change their hearts and even save them. There is only one time when you are allowed to not obey what they say and still be blessed by God, and that is if they ask or tell you to do something that is clearly sin, and displeasing to the Lord. In that case, you don't have to do it, though God does still expect you to be respectful in your refusal.

What if your parents have done something that really hurt you, and you just can't seem to get over it, and you don't want to respect them because of what they did? This is where forgiveness comes in.

Forgiveness

God has forgiven us so much! How can we hold back our forgiveness from others? He has forgiven us even though we killed His only Son, and though we continue to break His laws every day,

"Let all bitterness and wrath and anger and clamor and slander be put away from you, along with all malice. Be kind to one another, tenderhearted, forgiving one another, as God in Christ forgave you." Ephesians 4:31-32

We cannot let any root of bitterness or anger spring up in our hearts, because it is like a poison that eats away at us inside, and will destroy us as well as those around us if we aren't able to let it go and to forgive. *("Strive for peace with everyone, and for the holiness without which no one will see the Lord. See to it that no one fails to obtain the grace of God; that no "root of bitterness" springs up and causes trouble, and by it many become defiled..."* Hebrews 12:14-15)

"Put on then, as God's chosen ones, holy and beloved, compassionate hearts, kindness, humility, meekness, and patience, bearing with one another and, if one has a complaint against another, forgiving each other; as the Lord

has forgiven you, so you also must forgive. And above all these put on love, which binds everything together in perfect harmony. And let the peace of Christ rule in your hearts, to which indeed you were called in one body. And be thankful." Colossians 3:12-15

This verse holds some important keys to overcoming anger and bitterness and unforgiveness. First, forgiveness and love and kindness are things that we have to *choose* to "put on". They won't "just happen" – they take work and prayer and effort. Second, we must keep in mind, when someone has hurt us, how much God has forgiven us for…and that we must forgive others in the same unconditional way. Third, we must ask God to fill us with His love for each person, because His love can overcome struggles that we could never get through on our own. And Fourth, it's important not to get trapped in a self-pitying attitude of thinking of yourself as the "victim" and feeling sorry for yourself. Instead, "be thankful", and thank God for His many blessings even in the midst of the hardship, and thank Him for His goodness, and for all of the things you *do* appreciate about the person who has hurt you, etc.

One last thing that is important to keep in mind is that, *"…if you forgive others their trespasses, your heavenly Father will also forgive you, but if you do not forgive others their trespasses, neither will your Father forgive your trespasses."* Matthew 6:14-15

If we expect God to forgive us when we have sinned and messed up, He expects us to forgive others. And if we persist in unforgiveness, God will also not forgive us, which is a very sobering thought, and one that is worth pondering when you are tempted to hold onto a grudge or anger or bitterness.

So if you have recognized that you *do* have bitterness, or anger, or unforgiveness in your heart, take some time to pray, and bring it to the Lord, and confess it to Him. Ask for His help to forgive and to love and to overcome these things.

One other Biblical example is a story found in Matthew 18:21-35, which is well worth looking up and reading.

63

Put This To Action:

- Think back to the last time you were disrespectful to your parent(s). Ask for God's forgiveness and ask Him to remind you and help you not to do the same thing again.
- Pray and ask the Holy Spirit to search your heart and show you all the ways you haven't honored your parents, so you can repent.
  - Apologize to your parents for every time you were disrespectful outwardly.

- This week make it your goal to do all that you can to help and bless your parents. Pray for them every day, and ask God to give you ideas of how to bless them. Then…keep on doing it every week.
- Take time to search your heart for any unforgiveness or anger, and ask the Lord to help you to forgive – and then work towards complete forgiveness and love.

Letter 6:

Guys *or* God?

Dear Every-girl,

Guys *or* God?

Yes, it *actually* comes down to that; do you look to <u>guys</u> as your "savior" and best friend? Who is it that you think about all the time? Who is it that you want to please, and hope is noticing you? Who is it that you long to spend all of your time with? What is his name? Is it a guy...or is it God? It can't be both. When you read the Bible, you begin to understand that God is a jealous God; He wants His people to find their delight in Him, and not to be constantly looking to other things, expecting them to satisfy us...because He knows that *nothing* else can ever satisfy us like He does – and yes, this includes guys, too. God knows that if we chase after these other things, and if we let them consume our thoughts and hearts, we will end up empty, and hurt, and never satisfied, and missing out on the joy and peace and fulfillment that we could find if only we put all these other things aside in order to seek Him. He loves us and wants the best for us. And I love you too, and want to see you living your life full of joy and delighting in the Lord, which is why I'm saying these things. I've been through the "boy crazy" phase, and seen it run its course in many of my friend's lives. I thank the Lord often that He rescued me out of it quickly...but the lives of the friends I've had who are still stuck in it have become very empty.

It started out when we were pretty little, and we heard rumors of "crushes" and "cooties". We were young, and so of course what we heard began to shape the way we thought about certain things. It started innocently enough, and we had no real sinful thoughts or desires – we were just acting the way we thought we should, based on what we had heard. We adopted our "secret crushes" – the boys we each thought were the cutest or funniest or just plain fun to be around – and we'd talk about them in "secret" code words (though of course they were never as secret as we acted like they were...and we always held onto a little hope that maybe they *would* decipher the code, and find out we liked them). We didn't realize then that it was actually possible to love people with God's love, which means that we can hang out with them, and love them, but not get caught up in the trap the devil sets at such a young age, where our thoughts begin to be consumed with boys, and we begin to seek *their* attention, instead of seeking the Lord. (Are you beginning to understand that the devil will use *anything* to try to distract us from spending time with the Lord?) Every sleepover was spent talking all night about who we "liked" (or trying to pry it out of our friends), and why we thought that *maybe* they "liked" us too, and talking about what it would be like when we got married and sometimes being upset when we discovered someone else with the same crush. And every day we were around them was spent (though we wouldn't have admitted it) sending subtle hints to the person we liked that they were, in fact, our crush.

When our thoughts are consumed with thinking about guys (or one in particular), texting guys, talking to guys, talking to our friends about guys, chatting with guys online, and trying to make ourselves noticed by guys…well…not only does that not leave a whole lot of time for God, but it also is setting ourselves up for failure, because when we are so consumed with thoughts about guys and loving our relationships or desires for a relationship *more* than God, it is causing them to become a type of idol in our hearts, as I've discussed before, which is not ok with God. When you become a Christian, it's not just a label; it's a completely different and new life and way of living, which most people who aren't Christians won't understand. *They* may be consumed with the distractions of the world, but for the Christian, our job and *delight* is to live for Jesus alone. Living for any other thing is like, as Charles Spurgeon said, "committing a spiritual adultery"…or, in a more modern turn of phrase, it's like cheating on God. Colossians 3 says, *"If then you have been raised with Christ, seek the things that are above, where Christ is, seated at the right hand of God. Set your minds on things that are above, not on things that are on earth. For you have died and your life is hidden with Christ in God. When Christ who is your life appears, then you also will appear with him in glory. Put to death therefore what is earthly in you: sexual immorality, impurity, passion, evil desire, and covetousness, which is idolatry. On account of these the wrath of God is coming."*

The old part of us in fact has to die. And, when we become a Christian, God truly begins to transform and change our hearts and makes them actually new. He removes the old desires and replaces them with new desires. Being a Christian isn't about loving the world and everything in the world *plus* loving Jesus, too. We actually ought to become completely different from the world, and loving only Jesus, and *running* from everything that displeases the Lord. If your heart and mind are still consumed with thoughts about guys, and wanting guys to like you, and talking with all your friends about guys, and planning out your future based on guys, then you would do well to ask yourself if you are truly desiring the Lord: if your heart has really been changed by God for a new one, and if you are actually seeking the "things that are above". Guys should never EVER take the place of God in our lives. And, in fact, if we are really desiring to have our eyes fixed on the Lord, and to trust Him with our lives, we shouldn't even be thinking about guys at all in these ways, because there's no reason to. If we *really* trust God like we say we do, can't we trust Him to bring us the right guy at the right time and to make it clear to us, so that we shouldn't even have to "look around" for guys that "might work"?

I'm going to say one more thing that might surprise you, and those of you who have been justifying your "boy-craziness" by saying, "Well, they're *just friends*" may be annoyed…but I know this to be true in almost every case, which is why I'm saying it: It's almost impossible for a girl to have a "best friend" who is a guy, and not have her heart and emotions involved. The wisest thing for a girl who wants to be pure in heart to do is to actually determine that she will not let herself become too close in any friendship with a guy, to where she is sharing her dreams, struggles, desires and other topics that tend to make people feel closer than perhaps they should. These sorts of conversations should be had with trusted friends who are also girls, or with members of your own family, or just with God Himself. Some people will say I'm being silly and far too cautious. But I've been there, and I've seen that this is true. Talking about intimate things with a "guy-friend" causes your emotions to engage (even if that wasn't your intention), and most girls I have seen fall into this snare don't make it out without it drawing them into corruption and sin, and without their hearts being broken and their whole lives being thrown off track. It's also so easy in these cases for the girl to begin looking to her guy friend as a "savior" of sorts, and needing him to talk through things with and for the emotional comfort he brings...instead of simply bringing your struggles and fears to the Lord. If you really want to guard the other person's heart as well, and not cause any impure thoughts or false hopes to grow in them either, you will wisely consider what I am saying. Today in our own church youth groups, it is like a contest to see who can get closest to "the line" without technically crossing it. Girls will show up dressed as if they were trying to see who can dress the most seductively, without actually getting in trouble, and they will see how close they can get to a guy without breaking any real rules. The only guy aside from your family and the Lord that you should pour out your heart to is actually your husband. But you should not assume that any and every guy you befriend "might" be "the one", and so, feel justified in talking with them this way. He's not your husband until you say "I do" and the pastor pronounces you man and wife. And I have only great joy in knowing that I did not open up my heart to the man who is now my husband until he asked to court me, and we went on our first walk together beneath the fragrant flowering trees of springtime. I have only ever wished I had been able to save *more* for him; I've never regretted not letting myself get closer to my guy friends of the past.

I wanted to trust the Lord and not be leading guys' hearts astray, and I didn't want to give any of them false hope that maybe I liked them, and I just didn't want to be thinking much about them other than as strictly friends – I wanted to save as much of myself as possible for the guy the Lord was preparing for me to marry...so these are a few things I did throughout the years to keep myself from falling into any snares or traps, because it is so easy to be caught by them without even realizing it, especially with the modern technology and ways of communication we have:

-I would never start an online chat with a guy, unless it was strictly business-related. I had the same sort of standards with texting, and tried to limit my texting with anyone, so it wouldn't consume all of my time. (I also didn't tell any of my guy friends that I had set these standards, because that would have gone against the purpose of making them in the first place.)

-If I felt a guy was showing me too much attention online, I would just stop chatting with him, and would sometimes have to block him from seeing that I was online.

-I wouldn't chat with anyone at night, after a reasonable hour (9 or 10pm).

-I wouldn't go on a car ride alone with a guy (even if my own motives were pure, it was to avoid even the appearance of evil, and to not give the devil any room to work with).

-I never complimented a guy on his looks or strength or anything physical. Sometimes I would say things to encourage guys in their walk with the Lord though, or good character qualities.

-Whenever I was doing something with a guy, or talking to a guy, I would often stop and think to myself, "What would my future husband (who I don't know yet) think if he was here? Would he be jealous? Hurt? Sad? Would he be excited to have me tell him what I was just doing or saying?"

-"What about God? What would God think if He was sitting right next to me?"

The best thing you can do for any guy is to pray for him, and to step back and not think that you can change him yourself, and not to think of him as "yours", because he's not – he is God's. I also made a list of 40 things that I found as good character traits of guys in the Bible. I showed the list to some friends, and their first reaction was to laugh, because it seemed like an impossible list. They were quick to assure me that I wouldn't find a "perfect" guy, which I knew was true; no guy is going to be perfect or completely free from sins or vices. However, I also knew that, unless you set your standards high, you will fall for anything. And I decided to try to set mine as high as I could (but I wanted them to be based on the Bible, because I had some friends who made almost impossible lists of things that their guys had to do or look like before they would be in a relationship with them). And, though over the years, I got to the point where I was willing to overlook the list…it just so happened that the guy God had prepared for me also has nearly every godly quality on the list…which means it's not impossible, and it's not just for perfect people – these are things that God actually finds important. You can find this list in Appendix B, at the back of the book, if you'd like to study it yourself.

Relationships:

So, it all started with the crushes and the sleepovers with our girlfriends. But then, as we got older, into our teenage years, many of my friends began to have the mindset that they weren't normal if they didn't have a boyfriend. And then they began to feel as if they needed a boyfriend in order to find their security and love. Some fell for any guy who could say the words, "I love you" – even if he didn't actually have any idea what real love was…but they didn't either, because you can only discover the meaning and depth of real love as you get to know Jesus, because He *is* Love, and trying to find or give love apart from Him is a definite failure every time.

Many of them went to public school, and through the influences there, and the movies and music they had, they began to feel the almost irresistible pull of selfishness; feeling the desire to be loved, and always wanting more and more, and getting into things that God has intended to be only for people who have followed His commands, and who have gotten married, as he ordained. Unless the Lord gives you the strength, and your greatest desire is to obey the Lord's voice and to be pleasing in His sight, you too will be ensnared by the grip of selfishness. You may say you can resist its pull now…but will you in the moment of temptation? Real love, which I will go into greater detail about in a later letter, is about giving up your own desires to bless and serve the other person, looking out for *their* best interest. However, what the devil has deceived most people on earth today into believing is love actually is not love at all. It is a selfishness that says, "That's a cute guy…cute guys make my eyes happy…I want that guy to be mine." It says, "I'll make you happy as long as you are doing your best to make me happy…and if you stop or mess up, it's over." And it thinks, "I can do what I want, because it's *my* heart, and *my* body, and anyway, it makes *me* happy to have someone notice me, and pay me compliments, and give me the hugs I want, and do things with me so I'm not lonely."

So one large problem with the way almost everyone views relationships today is the selfishness and lack of real love. The real purpose for a relationship is two people coming together to prayerfully consider whether God would have them to get married, and it should only be started when both people are in a place in their lives where they could actually be married (in other words, a relationship between 15-year-olds is contrary to the true purpose of a relationship, because they can't even think of getting married for another 3 years at least). Any time before that, (before reaching a marriageable age, that is – 18 or older) and it will just be one long distraction for both of you. A relationship is not just to have fun – to get what you can out of it – or to feel loved. It is to determine if God would have you to get married…and sometimes it doesn't even take all too long to figure that out. Things like hugging, kissing, and holding hands are not things to be played around with. They are things which God blesses within marriage, but which only stir up lust and selfishness (things which go directly against God's design of what real love is supposed to be) when they are indulged in before any real commitment to marriage has been made. Many girls don't realize that it's possible to *not* do these things, because…well…*everyone* does them! But I can tell you that, before we were married, my husband and I chose not to hold hands until we were engaged, and not to kiss until our wedding day. Not only did these things help us to grow closer as friends without adding the element of lust to our relationship, but it made these things even sweeter when we were able to do them at last! Was it hard? Yes…it was very hard some days; there were days when all I wanted to do was hold Gabe's hand…but I would pray, and ask God to help me to trust Him and to wait, and I would tell Him that I knew His way would be sweeter…and I was not disappointed.

You might ask, "Well, how will I ever know who I want to marry unless I get to know a bunch of guys, so I can tell what I like and don't like about them?" That is a very common question I've been asked. And the truth is that it actually doesn't matter at all. First off, you get to see enough of guys in normal, day-to-day life and socializing to tell what you like and don't like about them. Secondly, when people go on dates, they are always trying to make themselves look as good as possible, and there are many people who have "dated around", and gotten married to someone who they thought was "the one", and then realized that this person was not really who they pretended to be. Thirdly, the more you spend time with the Lord, and the more time you spend reading the Bible, the more you will come to know and understand what a godly guy should act like, and the Lord will actually direct you in the way you should go if you just trust Him and have patience. When God brings the right guy along, you will be able to tell pretty simply, and all the crushes and dates of the past won't make any difference in your decision anyway, except that, if you skip them, you will have more of your heart left to give to the guy that God has provided to be your lifelong best-friend.

Another problem with it is that relationships are actually often used by the devil as 1.) a means of distracting us from the Lord (again), and 2.) a snare that leads many Christian girls away from the Lord, when not much else would.

I have had several Christian friends who really loved the Lord turn away from their relationship with Him and go down some very harmful paths in their lives because of relationships with guys who weren't Christians (the Bible actually says that a Christian should not marry someone who is not a Christian: 2 Corinthians 6:14, *"Do not be unequally yoked with unbelievers. For what*

partnership has righteousness with lawlessness? Or what fellowship has light with darkness?"), and they grew to love the guy more than the Lord…or because of relationships with guys who said they were Christians, but weren't really living like it, and who led the girls astray with many distractions…or because of relationships that they placed all of their hope on, which didn't work out, and they then began blaming God and not trusting that God had a plan in it all, and was working things out for their good. A relationship with a guy should never be as important to us as our relationship with the Lord. The Lord is always first priority. And God must be our foundation stone. If the guy you like isn't in love with God first and foremost, no matter how "cute" or "funny" or "nice" he is, he won't be able to love you rightly, because God *is* love, and because this guy's foundation won't be secure. Don't even consider marrying someone who doesn't care about honoring and pleasing the Lord more than he cares about you. (And this doesn't mean that he won't be able to love you, because once he cares about God most of all, God will fill him to overflowing with *His* love, and He will show the guy how he can bless you the most – more than he could on his own! And it's the same for you; don't even consider being in a relationship until you love God most, and only care about pleasing Him.)

Modesty and Femininity:

Girls are very emotionally-based, and we want people to like us, and we desire their admiration and acceptance. Even if you don't realize it, it's probably quite important to you. Many times, these desires will dictate how we act, dress, etc – *especially* as it relates to guys. We've become a society of "guy-pleasers". This is how most girls are. However, that does not mean that it's okay. It is a part of our nature that we actually need to take to the Lord in prayer and ask Him to change it in us. We must learn to desire to please only God, and we must determine to follow Him, no matter what anyone else thinks.

I'm not going to write a book on modesty at this point, because there are plenty of books on the topic out there, if you are interested in looking for them. And modesty is not really as complicated as people think it is. It's not about a list of do's and don'ts. It's not about you needing to always wear skirts and turtlenecks. It actually comes down to a matter of your heart attitude, and of your desires and motives. Take, for example, the illustration of a book:

A book is basically made up of two parts: the cover, and the pages inside. The cover makes the book look attractive; it's what makes you want to pick it up and read it or causes you to pass it by. If it's sturdy, it will also protect the pages. You never actually get to the pages until you've first seen the cover. The pages hold the most valuable and intriguing part of the book - its substance. Let's face it, you don't just buy the covers... *but* according to research, you're more likely to buy the book if it *has* a cover. Without the cover, the pages are going to fade, get stained, and fall apart much faster.

"Publishers pay for a book to be advertised in book stores with the cover facing out, because they know that the cover sells the product. Most children and adults are more likely to select an attractive looking book than one that is dull in appearance and gives no clue to its contents." -Vandergift

Like books, both the *outward* part of femininity and the *inward* part of femininity work hand-in-hand, and one isn't much good without the other. Granted, the pages of the book may be a bit more valuable than the cover, and what God does in our hearts is more important than what we wear or how we present ourselves...but I hope you can see with this illustration that the value of what's inside is greatly lessened (at least by a casual observer) by something wrong with the outside.

It's what goes on in your heart that makes you truly feminine. Wearing dresses, a smile, and flowers in your hair should all be an overflow of the joy you have within you, and the confidence you have from your identity being securely rooted in Christ. When that kind of joy and peace overflows from your heart, you'll look a lot more feminine than many women do today. Like a book with a jewel encrusted cover, it's what's on the inside that makes your countenance shine, and that's what makes you truly feminine.

If your clothing causes your brothers in Christ to stumble (whether or not you realize it), you are not bringing glory to God for what He's done in your life. You're like a book cover that has been soiled and ruined; people are going to have a hard time getting past that cover to see what lies within.

You might think, *Well, they'll have to get over it - that's just how I am, and I'm not ashamed of it. If they're too legalistic to get past how I look, I could care less about them.* If that's true of you, that's not where God wants you to stay. Bringing attention to yourself through improper dress might possibly cause others to look on the Cross of Christ in scorn, as they see that you are not really any different from any other desperate, hopeless girl out there who's flaunting everything she's got because she feels like that's the only way she'll ever be noticed.

When Christ changes your heart, you begin to realize that your goal in life is not to be noticed for your outward appearance, but to point others to the saving gospel of Jesus Christ. So ask yourself this question next time your look at yourself in the mirror. Are your choices of clothing a distraction? Do they agree with what the Bible says is suitable for a young woman professing to be a follower of Christ? *Are they drawing attention to you, or pointing to the Lord?*

Some people mistakenly believe that how you dress has nothing to do with femininity or being a Christian, while others mistakenly believe that wearing a dress is the *only* way you're Biblically feminine. So what does the Bible say? Let's take a look:

"Charm is deceitful and beauty is vain, But a woman who fears the Lord, she shall be praised." **Proverbs 31:30**

Flirting, attractiveness, allure, looks – they're all superficial and fleeting; they don't really *make* a woman; they don't make her feminine, or praise-worthy. What does? Fearing the Lord.

If we truly fear the Lord, we will keep His commandments with our whole hearts – forsaking all that distracts us from the Lord, and asking Him to reveal any idols we have allowed to remain in our lives – whether it be looking attractive, or the entertainment we enjoy, or worldly success and ambitions instead of seeking the Lord with *all* of our hearts. It is far too easy to pursue everything *but* the Lord. And these things will keep us from true beauty and Biblical femininity if we aren't earnestly and often asking the Lord to search our hearts.

"Those who look to him are radiant, and their faces shall never be ashamed." **Psalm 34:5**

The Lord Himself will make our faces radiant when we spend time in His presence. Spending time with the Lord is the most important part of becoming beautiful within - desiring Him more than anything else.

"Likewise, I want women to adorn themselves with proper clothing, modestly and discreetly, not with braided hair and gold or pearls or costly garments, but rather by means of good works, as is proper for women making a claim to godliness." 1 Timothy 2:9-10

This verse is showing us what's really important if we say we are respectable Christians - respectable meaning: "Meriting respect or esteem; Of or appropriate to good or proper behavior or conventional conduct." If we are respectable, we will delight in wearing modest clothing that doesn't shout, "Look at me!" but which quietly says, "I have self-control and God has given me joy in dressing in such a way that it does not draw attention to my body, but my heart."

Also, our adornment will not be merely wearing fancy hairdos or adorable clothes, but clothing ourselves in *good works*. I am convinced when we walk in the good works God has prepared for us, He looks down on us with a huge smile, because good works are more precious to Him than even a crown of rubies and pearls could ever be. We can't earn God's favor with good works, but when Christ has saved us, good works should be a natural outpouring of our hearts that have been filled with Christ's love. And sharing the joy and hope that Christ has placed in us with others is the most beautiful thing we could ever do.

"Search me, O God, and know my heart; Try me and know my anxious thoughts; And see if there be any hurtful way in me, and lead me in the everlasting way." Psalm 139:23-24

Finally, these verses remind us that we need to humbly come before God and ask the Holy Spirit to show us if there is anything in us that is grieving Him - anything that needs to change in our lives, and then be willing to obey. Maybe for you it might be something as simple as smiling more often, or maybe you need to learn how to act like a lady and not a selfish child. Maybe you need to go through your whole wardrobe and ask yourself *why* you wear each of the things you own… or maybe… just maybe, what you need most of all right now, more than a skirt or a dress, is to throw yourself before God, and find your identity in Him, to spend time with Him, and have Him instruct you in His good and perfect ways. That is where femininity starts.

Femininity (both inside and out) takes *cultivation:* "to promote or improve the growth of something by labor and attention; to develop or improve by education or training." So what are some things you can do to cultivate a feminine spirit? I suggest starting with prayer, reading the Bible, worshipping God, looking for ways to serve others, fellowshipping with other godly young women you know, and practicing a *gentle* spirit… Can you think of more?

Also, modesty should affect our speech as well – not just our outward appearance. What does it mean to be modest in our speech? It is the same thing as being modest in what we wear: What we say should point others to the Lord, and not draw attention to ourselves, or be displeasing to the Lord in any way. Ephesians 4:29 says, *"Let no corrupting talk come out of your mouths, but only such as is good for building up, as fits the occasion, that it may give grace to those who hear."* Is what you say encouraging to those around you? Does it fall under the classification of "graceful"? Unfortunately for all of us, the answer is all too often "No". Asking the Lord to guard your mouth, and to help you not say anything that it worthless or displeasing to Him is a great place to start. It takes a lot of work to change the way we talk, and what we talk about…but God will help us if we ask Him. And you don't have to be constrained to the meaningless babble that everyone expects of young ladies these days. You can actually be the one to direct conversations with your friends to useful and godly things when they begin to get off track (as they do so easily). Just pray and ask God to help you to be able to direct the conversation back to useful and good things instead of worthless things, and He will. You also don't have to be afraid to walk away from a conversation that is not honoring the Lord, especially when your friends don't want to change the topic. It may be difficult, and your friends might mock you…but God will honor you, and bless you for taking a stand for what is right.

A wonderful side-blessing of dressing and acting modestly is that it allows you to actually be able to be a real friend to guys! Guys who really love the Lord have a hard time just being friends with girls who dress and act immodestly, but when you are trying to please the Lord in these areas, it makes them feel much more comfortable around you, and they aren't always having to guard their eyes or struggle with their thoughts when they are talking to you, and it makes you able to have a much more real, and a far sweeter friendship with them.

Old Maids?

You might have wondered at some points of this letter, "So if I give up thinking about guys, and just seek the Lord, will I be an old maid? I want to get married *someday*!" or "Is wanting to be married wrong?" And the answer to both of those questions is, "Nope!" It again comes down to your heart attitude and motives. God may have plans for you to stay single, but He may be preparing someone for you to marry at this very second, just as He is preparing you for them. One of the most beautiful things about not taking matters into your own hands, but instead, just trusting the Lord, is that, when He does bring the right person into your life, you get to see that it was completely His plan, and that He is actually a far better matchmaker than we could ever be. Wanting to be married is not wrong, but wanting it so much that you aren't willing to give it up if the Lord asks you to *is* wrong…or if you spend too much time thinking about it, and find that you are unable to give it up because you don't fully trust the Lord to work out His good plan, then it may also be wrong. In the next chapter, I will share a part of my story of surrendering that desire to the Lord.

Put This To Action:

- What are the name(s) of the guy(s) you "like"? Write them down here if you are willing to give them to the Lord, and to not think of them as crushes any more (or potential boyfriends or husbands), but only as brothers in Christ and fellow soldiers for the Lord.
    - Pray and ask God to help you give them to Him...and then tell Him that you are giving these guys up for Him, and that you only want to be His, and to please Him.

_____

_____

- If you are in a relationship with a non-Christian, ask God for the strength to break up, because God asks us to not be in relationships with those who don't know Him...and they will only lead you astray – even if you think you can change them, that is something you just have to leave up to the Lord.
- Make a list of <u>at least</u> 3 things you can start doing to guard your heart and the hearts of your guy friends. Make them hard for yourself.

_____

_____

_____

- Go through your clothes and ask yourself if they are pointing to the Lord and telling those who look at you that you are His, or if they are drawing attention to yourself (or any particular body parts) and trying to get guys to look at you. Pray and ask God to show you what <u>He</u> thinks...and then throw out anything you think you should.

Letter 7:

Through The Fire

Dear Every-girl,

As I've just mentioned in the previous letter, sometimes it happens that God will test us. He'll send us through the fire of adversity to refine us or He'll confront us with a choice, and see what we do. (Remember the story of Daniel in Letter 4?)

God brought me face-to-face with a choice not too long ago, and it was actually one of the hardest things I've ever had to do. Though outwardly it probably seemed like everything was fine, inwardly there was a battle going on of epic proportions. I will share it with you, as I refer to my journal, though it's hard...but I'm sharing it because I believe that this might be able to give some of you a perspective that you've never thought about before on certain things...because I know I hadn't.

I will begin this tale by telling you that, for several days previous to what I am about to share, I was struggling a lot with my own desires - especially the desire to have a relationship, to be married, and to have a family. It was pretty much a constant struggle throughout the day, as I tried to take my thoughts and desires captive and give them to God. I was getting exhausted just trying to keep up with them! (What do I mean about "taking my thoughts and desires captive"? I mean that, every time one of them would cross my mind, I would give it to the Lord, and ask Him to take it from me and to help me keep my mind on Him. I would ask for His help not to think about those things any more, and every time I did, over and over again, I would say, "No, I am not going to think about these things. Jesus, please help me!" And He always does...though sometimes it's harder than others. Especially if you really actually want the things you are thinking about. It can take a lot of effort to resist the temptation to think about them.) Now, of course it's not wrong to desire any of these things, but when they begin to consume your thoughts and you spend all your time thinking about them, and you spend more time thinking about them than spending time with the Lord, and you actually begin to desire these things more than the Lord...well, then you can be quite certain that they have become a type of "idol" in your heart. God tells us that, "You shall have no other gods before me." (Exodus 20:3) And an idol in your life is *anything* that takes the place of God in your thoughts, time, heart, etc. Anything that's more important to you than spending time with the Lord, anything that replaces the time you could be spending with the Lord – all those things are "other gods", and letting them stay, and continuing to "worship" them instead of turning away from them goes directly against God's commandments.

Then I went to a Bible study, during which, I had a really nice time with the Lord…and the message was about the story in 1 Samuel, when the Ark of the Covenant was brought into the temple of Dagon, and about how the people of the town woke up the next morning, and their idol, Dagon, was on his face before the ark…and the point of the message was about how *our* idols have to fall before the presence of the Lord in our lives. It was an excellent study, and the leader brought up some of the big things that become idols for most Americans, like success and entertainment. But I had heard these things multiple times throughout the last few months, and wasn't particularly feeling like I personally was learning much of anything new. God had actually made it relatively easy (not just a piece of cake, but not as much of a struggle as it is for some people) for me to give up worldly movies and music and worldly success, because none of those things has held a particularly strong grip on me, compared to the joys of the Lord.

However, toward the end of the Bible study, one of the guys began to share about how he had been working to make sure that his whole life - all his plans, desires, and dreams - were surrendered to the Lord completely……and in that moment, when I least expected it, God was there beside me. He just suddenly opened my eyes and brought me face-to-face with the reality of what *actually* surrendering *everything* to Him could mean…and it was hard – really hard. God didn't confront me about any of those things which I had given to Him without even much of a second thought when He asked me to. Nope. He confronted me with the desires I have *said* I was surrendering to Him though I was really still holding onto them with the hope that my own desires were actually what *God* wanted for me, too…and so, I didn't fully surrender them, or even really understand what "fully surrendering" truly meant. He confronted me with the very thing I had been struggling with so much that very day… (which actually made what He was showing me that much more intense).

I suddenly realized that if I *actually* completely surrendered my desire for a relationship to the Lord, I was giving up having a lifelong closeness and intimate friendship with a guy, I was giving up ever having a first kiss or holding hands, I was giving up the security of having a husband to lead me and teach me and counsel me, I was giving up being able to serve God side-by-side with a husband, I was giving up having my own family……and all that was hard – incredibly hard, because my flesh wanted it so badly. And it was doubly hard because I knew that, despite all the joys of heaven, once I die, I will never again have the opportunity to be married, because things don't work quite like that in heaven…so if I give it up on earth, I give it up for good. But, I give it up for God.

And yet, I knew that this realization did not mean that God would *never* let me be married. He could yet bless me with that. But God brought me to this place of realizing all of these things, so that the full understanding of what He requires of me would fill me, and then He gave me a choice so that I would not be surrendering in words only, but in truth. I had to choose. I had to choose if I would look back; if those things were more important to me than serving God with all of my heart, soul, mind, and strength, or if I truly loved God *more* than life, and more than my own dreams and my strongest desires. I believe God made this so clear to me and showed me the full picture so that I could make a fully informed choice.

I sat there for what seemed like hours, though it couldn't have been…but I was wrestling with my own desires, with what God was showing me, and with all the pleasures the devil was laying before me, enticing my heart with. It felt like a tidal wave was pounding over me…and yet, as the roaring filled my ears, and the immense power nearly swept me off of my feet, God filled my mouth with the words, and my heart with the determination, and I said, *"Yes.* Yes, Lord, I will follow you no matter what it means. I will give up my life for you. All I am is yours. It's impossible for me to go back, or to live only *mostly* surrendered to you. Take my life, Lord, and use it in any way you can - any way you choose. It's all yours."

So, it was a very sobering night for me…and the next few days I was in a rather serious state of mind. But at the same time, I was rejoicing that the Lord caused my heart to be able to say "Yes" to Him in the midst of the strongest of desires and dreams and doubts pulling at my heart.

I didn't know where the Lord would use me, or how…but I knew that He was my Beloved, and there was nothing and no one else in this world that could ever be more worthy of my love and my life. There could be no turning back. And I knew that even if God did ever bring me into a marriage relationship, it would be for His glory and not for myself…and it could never be more important to me than Him anyway.

Zechariah 13:9 says, *"And I will put this third into the fire, and refine them as one refines silver, and test them as gold is tested. They will call upon my name, and I will answer them. I will say, 'They are my people'; and they will say, 'The LORD is my God.'"*

So as you can see from these verses, God will often test us to see where our hearts really are, and to see if we love Him as much as we say we do. These times may be difficult for you to understand, especially when the Lord asks you to give him something that is very important to you, as He did with me in the story I shared. But you must remember and trust that the Lord is testing you for your own good, because He loves you, and he sees the things in your heart that are actually harmful to you, and wants you to be free of them. He is refining you like silver; He must put some heat under you and melt you down in order to remove the impurities that are keeping you from the purity and beauty that He desires you to have. He wants to burn away your bonds, as in the story of Shadrach, Meshach, and Abednego.

When you give these things up to the Lord, it will probably hurt...and if you *think* you have surrendered them to the Lord, but found it to be easy and no big deal, there's a good chance that you haven't actually completely surrendered it...because God's refining and cleaning of our hearts, as He burns these wrong thoughts and pursuits out of us, can be quite painful when we've really gotten it *all* removed and extracted from us. After the pain, though, comes such a sweet closeness with the Lord and a joy that is beyond compare, and you don't even remember the pain anymore, because of the new sweetness of the Lord's presence.

But you know what the *most* special thing is? Jesus, the Master Shepherd, the King of Kings himself has called us - each of us - to follow him by name. Just take a moment to think about that. It is so amazingly special- that He Himself has called us and set us apart for Himself! May we live in a manner that is pleasing to Him. And may we serve Him with a joy that is befitting the amazing grace He has shown us, and the privilege He has given us of serving Him, and being used by Him.

I think it would be fitting to end this letter with some of the words to a song which beautifully reflects the heart attitude that we should be desiring and asking the Lord for:

"Take all I am, Lord
And all that I cling to
You are my Savior
I owe everything to
Take all the treasures
That lie in my storehouse
They cannot follow
When I enter Your house....
And I surrender all to You;

I surrender all."

(Ending note: I will mention that God actually saw fit to bring my future husband along within a month of the day when He helped me to surrender that desire completely to Him and to move forward in service to Him whether or not I would ever be married. So now, as I write this, a year later, I am married to a man whose heart is the Lord's, and whose character is far above all that I could have hoped for or prayed for or chosen for myself. And God had also asked him to surrender his own desires in much the same way just the year before. God's timing is perfect...and He makes a far better match maker than you or I ever could!)

Put This To Action:

- What do you think it means to actually surrender <u>everything</u> to the Lord? Are you willing?

Letter 8:

Love Like Death

Dear Every-girl,

So now that I've told you that, "what the devil has deceived most people on earth today into believing is love actually is not love at all", you may be wondering what real love actually is. I do not profess to be an excellent example of what real love is. I am weak, and sinful, and fail in this area quite often. But I know Jesus, and He not only is the best and most perfect example of what love really is...but He *is* Love. He is the very definition of love. So we should always look to Him as our example of what love is, as Ephesians 5:1-2 says, *"Therefore be imitators of God, as beloved children. And walk in love, as Christ loved us and gave himself up for us, a fragrant offering and sacrifice to Christ in God."*

I have wrestled through the writing of this letter quite a bit, and spent much time praying for God's wisdom on what to write, because it is actually a *very* important thing to understand rightly. I want you to be able to understand God's love, because if you understand His love correctly, it will transform your relationship with the Lord, and you will come to see and understand His goodness, and that He is much more selfless and humble and kind than we often think of Him...and it will also transform your relationship with others, if you take the Ephesians 5 verses to heart, and begin to work and pray toward imitating the love that you begin to understand that Christ has shown us.

You may be surprised to discover that love is not really an emotion that "just happens". It's not something that suddenly you "fall into". Love is partly emotion, but is actually also both *a choice* and *an action*.

God's Love For Us:

God's love is so perfect, and ours is so imperfect that it can be a hard thing to wrap our minds around and really believe. But it's such a beautiful thing to think about and to try to imitate, even if we can't fully understand it. *"...that you may....know the love of Christ that surpasses knowledge, that you may be filled with all the fullness of God."* Ephesians 3:14-19 (summarized)

The last part of the Ephesians 5 scripture is a good place to start in our exploration of love: *"And walk in love, as Christ loved us and gave himself up for us, a fragrant offering and sacrifice to Christ in God."* What is this verse saying? It is saying that Jesus Christ loved us so much that His love was displayed in a completely selfless action – the *most* selfless of actions; giving up his very life on our behalf. This action went hand-in-hand with His love for us, and it was a beautiful sacrifice. Philippians 1:27a says, *"Only let your manner of life be worthy of the gospel of Christ."* What is the gospel? The gospel, in short, is that Jesus Christ came to earth in the form of a man in order that He might take the penalty for our sins, so that we could be set free from the curse of sin, and become God's children forever. There was no reason that God had to do this for us. We humans certainly gave Him no reason ourselves; there is nothing delightful or good about us on our own, for, without the Lord, we are full of sin and continually run to the darkness. And yet, this is the wonder of wonders: *"For while we were still weak, at the right time Christ died for the ungodly. For one will scarcely die for a righteous person – though perhaps for a good person one would dare even to die – but God shows his love for us in that while we were still sinners, Christ died for us."* (Romans 5:6-8) Jesus loved us and was willing to sacrifice His own life for us – who are less than nothing in comparison with the King of the universe! – even though we had shown Him no love in return. Even though we are sinful and scoff at His good commands...yet, He has such great love for us and compassion on us that He would die even for those who were His enemies!

God's love for us is completely selfless, expecting nothing in return. So, in short, the gospel *is* love on display! So, in order that our manner of life may be worthy of the gospel, we must also walk in such love.

I've also seen illustrations of God's love through my husband, which have helped me to understand God's love for us better, in a more comprehensible way. On one of these occasions, Gabe said to me, "I love it when you come to sit beside me just because you like being with me. It really means a lot." In the same way, God Himself longs to spend time with us, His children whom He loves, and yet so often we are distracted by so many other things that we don't even realize He's sitting there just hoping we'll stop and sit with Him. Think of how much it thrills him and causes His heart much joy if, instead of doing something else, we choose to just sit with Him…just because we want to be with Him.

You might be tempted to wonder, "Does God <u>really</u> love me? It doesn't seem like He does." We all struggle with this thought now and then.

When was the last time you saw a sunset? If it wasn't recently, make it a point to go out and watch the sun set in the next day or two. When was the last time you heard a bird chirp, or felt a gentle breeze on your face? When was the last time that you read the Bible, and were encouraged by a verse? When was the last time you ate a meal, or laid down in a bed, or woke up to sun streaming through the window? When was the last time you spent time with the Lord, and just felt full of joy and peace? These are all proofs of God's love for you; all shouting that it's true. We must take hold of it firmly in faith when these sorts of doubts fill our minds. It is not because of anything we've done that God loves us, but because of His mercy. And if you feel like He can't love you because you've just messed up too badly….well, it's not true. Romans 8:1-2 says, *"There is therefore now no condemnation for those who are in Christ Jesus. For the law of the Spirit of life has set you free from the law of sin and death."* Jesus doesn't only love those who have never messed up. In fact, He came specifically for those who had "messed up" the worst, because, *"Those who are well have no need of a physician[doctor], but those who are sick."* Matthew 9:12b. All God asks of us is that we would come before Him humbly and confess our sins, and tell Him that we're sorry…and this enables Him to pour out His storehouses of love on us without measure, as He so longs to do but can't when we refuse to confess our sins, because He doesn't want to encourage or reward ungodly, prideful behavior - that would be very bad for our souls. But He just loves to be able to show His love for us…even especially when we don't deserve it, because it displays the greatness of His character.

One last thing you should keep in mind is to not doubt His love for you. If you doubt God's love for you, it's just the same as if someone you love a lot didn't believe you when you told them that you love them - it would really hurt. And it hurts God even more when we disbelieve His love for us, because He loves so much deeper than we ever could…and the one who loves the most is able to be hurt the most.

Our Love For Others:

Now that we have had a little glimpse into God's heart of love towards us…what should love look like in our own lives? First, we will take a look at a few verses:

"Beloved, let us love one another, for love is from God, and whoever loves has been born of God and knows God. Anyone who does not love does not know God, because God is love. In this the love of God was made manifest among us, that God sent his only Son into the world, so that we might live through him. In this is love, not that we have loved God but that he loved us and sent his Son to be the propitiation for our sins. Beloved, if God so loved us, we also ought to love one another." 1 John 4:7-11

"By this we know love, that he laid down his life for us, and we ought to lay down our lives for the brothers. But if anyone has the world's goods and sees his brother in need, yet closes his heart against him, how does God's love abide in him? Little children, let us not love in word or talk but in deed and in truth." 1 John 3:16-18

"This is my commandment, that you love one another as I have loved you. Greater love has no one than this, that someone lay down his life for his friends." John 15:12-13

The common core of these verses and of the gospel itself (which, you'll remember we discovered is actually the very essence and definition of love) is laying down our lives. This is the key to knowing the difference between real love and just emotions. This is also what makes real love so unpopular today, and it's why the Hollywood version of love is eagerly accepted - no one really wants to give up their own desires and expectations to bless and serve someone else, without any thought of getting anything in return. The common underlying expectation in relationships today is, "What's in it for me? What will I get out of it?" But the fact is that *real* love is completely selfless, and doesn't expect anything in return, and would, in fact continue to do its best to bless and serve the other person whether or not they ever said, "Thank-you," or even noticed.

Many people look at that standard of love, and not only does it *not* seem very fulfilling to them, but it looks nearly impossible. That is because it *is* impossible unless the Lord teaches it to us, and gives it to us Himself...*because real love can only come from God.* Real love goes against all of our natural human desires to be loved and served ourselves, because real love is a commitment to serve someone else and to do all that you can to bless *them*, whether or not they deserve it or ever do anything in return. *Real love means dying.* As Jesus displayed His love for us by actually dying on a cross, to take the punishment on Himself – punishment that we never could have paid – for our sins, so we, also, can only display real love when we die to our own desires and expectations.

The verses in 1 John, say that the definition of love is giving up your life for someone else...even if they don't return your sacrifice, or appreciate it. We actually have to die: to ourselves, our own desires, our own agendas, our own ideas of what comforts we want or "deserve" in this world...even dying to the false ideas that the world has given to us about what love looks like and what a "good" life on earth looks like! And then we must also give away what remains of our existences on earth to serve Christ...because we love Him...because we want others to love Him...and because anything else we do with our lives while on earth is meaningless in comparison to Christ and being with Him for eternity. Whew! It's no wonder that selfishness, in all of its many various forms, has become widely accepted as the new "love"! The *real* thing is *hard*! It is hard because our flesh and our sinful and fleshly desires must die...and that is never a pleasant thing for our selfishness to feel...BUT it is oh, so worth it, to our spirits, which will be soaring to new heights in the love of the Lord! And anything we sacrifice on earth will be repaid many times greater in heaven, when it will actually really matter.

A large portion of living life is really all about learning how to love others as Jesus loves them, because Jesus is teaching us how to be good citizens of heaven even now while we are still on earth. And I am continually praying that God would help me to love people like He loves them - giving up my life for them – whatever that may mean for me (whether in "small", daily sacrifices, or even *actually* giving up my life). And that He would reveal more of the truth of what love really is to me, and teach me how to show that love to others. I'm still a work-in-progress, as we all are. But when we really want to change and grow in this area, and learn what really loving someone actually means, God will truly begin to change us. And, like I said, *really* loving people (more than ourselves) is a hard thing. Something which we, in our human-ness are simply incapable of on our own. BUT...fortunately, we have the BEST teacher in matters of love that EVER existed; the One who created love Himself!

But for now, *"...that I may know him and the power of his resurrection, and may share his sufferings, becoming like him in his death..."* Philippians 3:10

Put This To Action:

- Next time you go out to pray, remember to thank God for His love for you.
- How does knowing the depth of God's love for you affect how you will love others?

_____
_____
_____
_____
_____
_____
_____
_____
_____

- Have you been upset with God or blaming Him for things and doubting that He really loves you? Apologize and get it right with God.
- Write down one thing you want to put in practice right away from this letter:

_____
_____
_____
_____

- What are some ways you can give up your life for your family and friends (and even enemies)?

_____
_____
_____
_____
_____
_____
_____
_____

Letter 9:

In All The World I Most Want...Nothing.

Dear Every-girl,

Matthew 7:24-27 says, *"Everyone then who hears these words of mine and does them will be like a wise man who built his house on the rock. And the rain fell, and the floods came, and the winds blew and beat on that house, but it did not fall, because it had been founded on the rock. And everyone who hears these words of mine and does not do them will be like a foolish man who built his house on the sand. And the rain fell, and the floods came, and the winds blew and beat against that house, and it fell, and great was the fall of it."*

What Jesus is talking about in these verses, is that, when we hear God's words or read God's words in the Bible and *do* them; if we take hold of Jesus' salvation by faith, and if we begin to take action and obey what Jesus is asking us to do, *this* is a solid foundation for our lives that will not be swept away by the storms of life (remember the previous letter on "storms"?) – our faith in the Lord will not crumble in those storms and trials, *if* we *act* on God's words. This is the good foundation. Now, in the next few verses, Paul goes on to talk about how we build on this foundation…

1 Corinthians 3:10-15 says, *"According to the grace of God given to me, like a skilled master builder I laid a foundation, and someone else is building upon it. Let each one take care how he builds upon it. For no one can lay a foundation other than that which is laid, which is Jesus Christ. Now if anyone builds on the foundation with gold, silver, precious stones, wood, hay, straw— each one's work will become manifest, for the Day will disclose it, because it will be revealed by fire, and the fire will test what sort of work each one has done. If the work that anyone has built on the foundation survives, he will receive a reward. If anyone's work is burned up, he will suffer loss, though he himself will be saved, but only as through fire."*

So what are these verses saying? Well, as I mentioned above, I believe that these verses are saying that, for all of us who are Christians, we should have only one foundation, which is Jesus. To become a Christian – a follower of Christ – of course, we cannot believe in any other thing. The beginning of Christianity is believing in Jesus alone, and His salvation. So, that is the foundation of our lives. But, throughout the rest of our lives, we have the opportunity to "build" on this foundation. And how do we build on it?

Everything we do is like a building block of our life…and we have the choice of picking good, solid building blocks, or of using flimsy, weak ones.

Each time we learn something new from a sermon or book or podcast that is true, each time we study God's Word, each time we help someone, each time we give up doing something that's "fun" in order to spend more time with the Lord, each time we talk to someone about Jesus – these are all things we can do that are like the building blocks and the framework of our lives, built on the foundation of Jesus…and they are all good things. However, there are also many things that are not as good, and do not make very good "building" materials…things like hearing teaching that is not Biblical and accepting it as true anyway without testing it by what the Bible says, spending our time watching movies or playing video games or going online (instead of studying the Bible or praying or other godly uses of time)…pursuing worldly goals and dreams, talking to our friends about movies or books or guys instead of about

Jesus, etc. Every time we do these sorts of things, it is like adding another block to the mansions of our lives. However, some of the blocks are made out of hay and sticks, while others are made out of rubies and emeralds. Now, what do you think will happen when we stand before the throne of Jesus when we die, and He judges what we've done with our lives by testing the mansion we've built with fire? If He sets our mansion on fire to test it, what is going to happen to it? The parts that were built with worthless things – the hay and sticks – will be burnt up, and any good parts they might be touching will fall down, causing the whole structure to be unstable. In the same way, if we aren't careful what we build with, not only will our eternal inheritances be at stake, but so will our earthly lives. If we waste our time with worthless things that won't last, our lives will be unstable as well, and empty – even though we may know Jesus. Just *knowing* Jesus isn't enough to bear good fruit (Matthew 7:17-20) or to store up our treasures, not on earth, but in heaven (Matthew 6:19-21). We must also *live our lives for Him*, if we have any desire of finding fulfillment, joy, and getting to heaven with more than just our bare skin. I know that I desire to have crowns that I can lay at Jesus' feet, because He is so glorious and worthy of all honor, and any little things I may be able to do to honor Him will never seem like enough to praise Him for His goodness, and all that He's done. (Note: God also will, at times, send trials and "fires" – sometimes real, and sometimes figurative – to help us to see the silliness of pursuing things of this world.)

For these reasons, we must be very careful about how we build on our foundation. Now, there are many lies in this world, and even in our churches and circles of "Christian friends" which the devil makes seem very attractive to us girls, and many girls are being completely led astray by them, into lives that are empty and filled with chasing after all kinds of things that won't last. I would like to mention just three of them here, because these lies (or bad building blocks) are very subtle, and you may be believing them or living in the way that they encourage without even realizing it. They are serious enough to completely sidetrack your life, and to cause you to stand before the Lord at the end of your life, in the brilliance and complete holiness of His presence with nothing to show for your life on earth except a smoking pile of ashes. Did you know that your life on this earth - talents, skills, time, singleness, marriage, money, etc.,- has actually just been loaned to you so that you can use them to show the world that Jesus Christ is the Lord, and that He longs to rescue sinners? It's true. And it's the *only* thing that really actually matters, and the only thing that will bring forth good that lasts even into all of eternity…and, because of that, serving the Lord is the only thing that can really, truly, actually satisfy us. (And it is the only thing that will give us building blocks of rubies and pearls which will not be destroyed when the Lord goes over what we've done with our life with the fire of testing.)

Every other pursuit requires constant striving and chasing after more notice and a better position and more money and all kinds of things and desires like these which can never actually be satisfied on earth. Even the person who *looks* like they have it all (the best house, nicest car, most money, best boyfriend)...they aren't satisfied or content, and they never will be, because contentment only comes from chasing after the one thing that matters – which is serving Jesus, and saving lost souls.

Lie #1 – The Dream-Big Delusion:

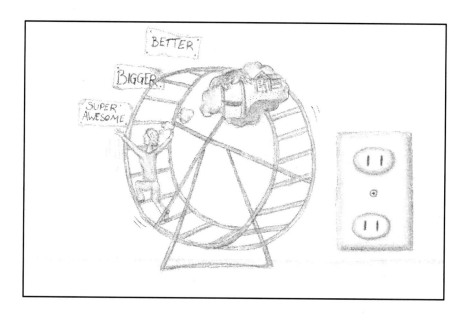

This first lie is one of the most attractive sounding lies you will ever hear. You will be told to "dream big", and then go after your dreams at any cost: "You shouldn't let anyone or anything get in your way or deter you from what you deserve." You are told that you should go after the Florida beach house you're dreaming of, you are told to strive for the "care-free" lifestyle where anything you want can be had, you are told to work towards being the "most

107

successful" nurse or actress or artist, etc. It all sounds great, right? Why *not* dream big, and go after the biggest and best of everything?

There isn't actually anything inherently and totally wrong with having a nice house or car or the ability to relax. What is so bad about this way of living then? Well, first it is the attitude of selfishness (and pride) behind it which begins to fill our hearts, and the way it causes our life focus to be completely on ourselves and what we want instead of others. (Philippians 2:4 says, *"Let each of you look not only to his own interests, but also to the interests of others."*) Second, it is totally opposite to the way Jesus lived and asked *us* to live (and, I don't know about you, but I desire for God to make me as much like Jesus as is possible). Jesus said, *"If anyone would come after me, let him deny himself and take up his cross and follow me. For whoever would save his life will lose it, but whoever loses his life for my sake and the gospel's will save it. For what does it profit a man to gain the whole world and forfeit his soul? For what can a man give in return for his soul?"* (Mark 8:34-37) Jesus is saying here that, if we want to truly follow Him, and be His disciples, we must *deny* ourselves and our own interests – we must be willing to give up our ideas of a "successful" life in this world for the sake of the gospel, in order to serve the Lord and love Him rightly. (It's that dying to our own desires thing again, like I talked about in the letter on love.) That is the only thing that can save our souls from being lost along with the rest of the world, who cares nothing about Jesus, and only wants to build up treasures for the short time they are on earth. If we choose, like them, that serving the Lord is not good enough for us, and we go after the world and all of its short-lived, fleeting pleasures and treasures, our lives will be sucked away into the vortex of continually seeking after these things, and striving for them, and we will be so consumed with ourselves and *our* success, that when we get to the end of our lives, and look back, what will be there? Will any of these things mean much to us in the end? Will there be anything truly lasting? Anything of real value? And what will Jesus say as we stand before Him on Judgment Day, if we have just spent our whole lives chasing after things that are worthless, instead of serving Him, and wanting to bless Him? What will we say to Him after we have spent our whole lives not even giving Him an hour out of our whole day, because all the other things of the world were more important to us? What will we say as He looks deep into our eyes, and we stand before Him with nothing to show for all of our years on earth except "things" that will be piles of dust when He wipes the earth clean of all its sinfulness, and makes it new? Spending our lives to have a better car, or to simply "pay the bills", or to be "comfortable", or to get new phones and iPods and computers, or to have better clothes, or nice vacations…all these things will seem completely absurd and worthless when we stand before Jesus empty-handed, and He asks us why He should let us into heaven.

1 John 2:15-17 says, *"Do not love the world or the things in the world. If anyone loves the world, the love of the Father is not in him. For all that is in the world—the desires of the flesh and the desires of the eyes and pride of life—is not from the Father but is from the world. And the world is passing away along with its desires, but whoever does the will of God abides forever."*

These verses are saying that you can't love the world or the things in the world, because everything that goes with them is opposed to God's heart...so, you can't love both God *and* the world – you must pick one or the other. The world and all its enticing-looking pleasures are going to end; all those things are only temporary, and don't really offer us anything that lasts forever. Have you ever noticed that money, happiness, security, etc., gotten from things of the world doesn't last forever? It doesn't. If you could find never-ending happiness in a boyfriend...why would girls go through so many? Or if you could get happiness from money itself, why would you ever spend it on a million different things, but to continually be looking for new things to try to "make you happy"? And what happens when the new, beloved, shiny car gets a dent, or catches on fire (as I had a car do once)? Where is your happiness then? Or when the boyfriend dumps you, or the money is stolen or becomes unavailable, or your computer stops working...what then? So you see, all of these things don't last, and can't give us a happiness that lasts. BUT, doing God's will, serving the Lord and bearing eternal fruit lasts forever! Ministering to people's souls and rescuing them from the pathway to hell, being focused on helping *others* rather than being focused on our own desires – these things will bring forth joy and peace and contentment that the things of the world can't even come close to. And they will last forever.

One last note in addition to this: These days, being "only" a mother is completely scorned and looked down upon, and the children are being sold out to the world and raised by their public school teachers and their peers, while their mom is out pursuing her dream life. These things should not be so! If you have children, or one day hope to have children, this is actually one of the highest callings a woman could ever have: to raise children who love the Lord. So, despite the culture's expectations, and despite how you've been raised and taught, take this matter to the Lord in prayer. I have been greatly blessed to have had a mother who was willing to stand against the culture and all of the criticism she got, and to be "only" a stay-at-home mother. She taught my brother and I all of our years of schooling, and I was so blessed to have continually been pointed to the Lord, and His Word. She sacrificed her "career", but her sacrifice has brought forth eternal fruit. And I know that any fruit my life bears will be credited to her, because of her great love for me.

Lie # 2 – Self-esteem Syndrome:

This lie is becoming more and more widespread today, *especially*, it seems, in church circles. It sounds good to us because it's everything we ever wanted to think about ourselves...and we are *encouraged* to do this! What could be better?! We are encouraged to love ourselves, and told that we must be able to do this successfully in order to ever be truly successful at anything else. We are told that we need to think positively about ourselves (because our self-esteem is very delicate), and we need to tell ourselves that we are strong, independent, assertive, beautiful, lovable, etc., and to chase after those things. We are told that we need to realize how much we deserve to be loved by God and by others…and that, in fact, we should put ourselves and our needs and desires first.

But the truth is that those things aren't what we need to be thinking about at all! Our human nature already naturally leans toward pride and having a haughty view of ourselves quite easily…we certainly don't need any help with it! Encouraging "self-esteem" is the same thing as encouraging pride. And pride is the very thing which caused Satan to be cast out of heaven, and it's the very opposite of all that Jesus did and said. Imagine you are given an amazing gift by one of your friends. Would you appreciate the gift and be filled with love toward the one who gave it to you more if you felt that you *deserved* the gift, or would you appreciate it more if you knew that you hadn't done anything to deserve the gift, and yet, they decided to give it to you anyway? Well, if you're like most people, I'm guessing you would be much more excited about the gift and blessed by it if someone decided to give it to you *even though you didn't do anything to deserve it,* just because they loved you. And your feelings toward them would be much more grateful and filled with love as well, than they would be if someone only gave you a gift because of something you did, and you were expecting it, and *knew* that you deserved it. (You might even look at it and think it wasn't quite good enough!) In the same way, each of us humans are completely sinful and have done nothing to deserve the love of a God Who is perfectly pure and holy; He has never had even the hint of a wrong motive or a sinful deed – ever! As I mentioned in the previous chapter, *"For while we were still weak, at the right time Christ died for the ungodly. For one will scarcely die for a righteous person – though perhaps for a good person one would dare even to die – but God shows his love for us in that while we were still sinners, Christ died for us."* (Romans 5:6-8) In order to see ourselves rightly, and to truly understand the richness and depth of God's love, these verses must really sink into our hearts. If we *deserve* to be loved because of our "innate goodness", then God's love really means nothing. *But,* if all is as the Bible says it is, then we are actually all sinners, worthy of eternal separation from the holy God and everlasting judgment for rebelling against His laws and commands…and yet, for no reason other than His perfect love, which is not based on anything we've done or could ever do (and, in fact, is because of Him choosing to overlook our sinfulness), God has reached out His arm of grace and pulled us out of our empty lives, and set our feet on the path of Life. He is so good!

So what else does the Bible have to say about this topic?

Luke 16:15 says, *"And he said to them, 'You are those who justify yourselves before men, but God knows your hearts. For what is exalted among men is an abomination in the sight of God.'"*

This is Jesus talking in this verse, and He very clearly states that what we exalt and highly esteem (including ourselves, as is the situation He's addressing in this chapter of Luke) is disgusting to God. Why?

Philippians 2:3-8 says, *"Do nothing from selfish ambition or conceit, but in humility count others more significant than yourselves. Let each of you look not only to his own interests, but also to the interests of others. Have this mind among yourselves, which is yours in Christ Jesus, who, though he was in the form of God, did not count equality with God a thing to be grasped, but emptied himself, by taking the form of a servant, being born in the likeness of men. And being found in human form, he humbled himself by becoming obedient to the point of death, even death on a cross."*

Jesus is completely humble, and it's not something we often think about…but when we actually meet God, I think we will be amazed and very surprised to see how incredibly humble He is. And when we are prideful and arrogant and think of ourselves as something special, it is disgusting to God, who is actually the only one who has a right to be proud…and yet, He chooses not to because He is so good. And how hurtful do you think it is to God when we think of ourselves as something special and when we think that we deserve His love because of how special and good we are, instead of just accepting His love as the amazingly generous and undeserved gift that it is? How would you feel if you bought your friend a new ipod just because you like them and wanted to be nice, and they grabbed it from your hand and said, "It's about time! I've been your friend for years, and you haven't given me a new ipod until now?!" That would not be a very nice feeling, especially after you probably spent a lot of money on this gift for them. But how do you think God feels when we have the same attitude toward Him about His gift of salvation? His heart is broken even deeper than ours could ever be, because He loves so much deeper than we can ever love.

Here is one more teaching from Jesus about this topic: *"He also told this parable to some who trusted in themselves that they were righteous, and treated others with contempt: 'Two men went up into the temple to pray, one a Pharisee and the other a tax collector. The Pharisee, standing by himself, prayed thus: "God, I thank you that I am not like other men, extortioners, unjust, adulterers, or even like this tax collector. I fast twice a week; I give tithes of all that I get." But the tax collector, standing far off, would not even lift up his eyes to heaven, but beat his breast, saying, "God, be merciful to me, a sinner!" I tell you, this man went down to his house justified, rather than the other. For everyone who exalts himself will be humbled, but the one who humbles himself will be exalted."* (Luke 18:9-14 ESV)

In this story of Jesus', He talks about a Pharisee who had a lot of self-esteem, and a tax-collector who was humble and thought of himself as only a sinner. The Pharisee thought he was a good guy, and that God was pleased with him and all of his good deeds. He trusted in His own goodness to make Himself pleasing to the Lord, instead of realizing that it is the act of humbling ourselves and throwing ourselves on the mercy of God that He looks with favor on, just as the tax collector did.

May we follow the example of our humble savior, Jesus, and the tax collector.

Lie #3 – The Fairytale Fog:

    Last, but not least, we have a very sneaky lie indeed, which creeps into our hearts often without anyone specifically saying anything to us about it. With this deception, we are led to believe that we ought to have something about us that is extraordinary, that other people will see and praise us for and love us for. We want to be special, and to have something about us that makes us stand out from everyone else as being lovable and desirable and unique. Many times, this desire takes root in us in a way we wouldn't really expect. Often, it begins to grow in our lives when we read a book or watch a movie with a main character who we really identify with (or even a real-life "star"), and who seems to have the "ideal" life – the boyfriend we long for, the adventure we crave, the family we wish we had, the fame we desire, the life-purpose that we're still looking for, the beauty we can only dream of, etc. And we see these characters, and begin to think, "If this character that I relate to so well had these things, why can't I?"

We begin to look at life through the eyes of this character in an attempt to be more like them, and may begin to think, "What would *this* person do in this situation?" And we begin to change our mannerisms or habits or things that we enjoy to match the things that this person or character does. We do all of this trying to be like this character we relate to in order that maybe we can find the same fulfillment and "happiness" that *they* found in *their* lives. Meanwhile, we end up being so totally focused on ourselves, and focused on finding fulfillment for ourselves that we waste all of our time day-dreaming and working to make ourselves more like these characters so that, in a "magical" moment, maybe our lives will end up being like theirs, and we forget about trying to help the people around us, and we forget about spending time with the Lord and seeking to please *Him*. If we don't bring these things to the Lord when we are young and ask Him to change us and learn from them, they will follow us all throughout the rest of our lives, though they may change slightly and take on forms other than trying to imitate a movie character, it is still the same root problem. And what *is* the root problem? The desires to be worshipped, esteemed, loved, prosperous, etc. – all these things come from pride. And pride is one of the most subtle and also the most dangerous sins. It is the sin that Adam and Eve first committed in the Garden of Eden…and it is still ingrained in us today.

Before I get ahead of myself though…my mother struggled with these things quite a bit when she was younger, so I asked if she would share some of her story with you:

"Laying out in green fields of grass, with wildflower scents carried by the breezes that were blowing the fluffy clouds across the azure screen where I played out my imaginations by the hour, seemed so harmless and well, wholesome. I wasn't doing anything bad, I had all my chores done and this was just 'me' time.....my escape from the reality of.....me. I fantasized hours of my young life away.

The mirror told me I wasn't anything special, I was rather affection starved and my schoolmates pretty much all excluded me from the events I heard about afterwards that they had done together. I wouldn't have been allowed anyway…

I wanted so badly to be special; to have something about me that would beguile and intrigue people and make them want to be with me. I studied girls in school who were popular and tried to mimic their mannerisms and fashion. When that didn't get me any more friends than I'd had before, I began to lie. I imagined the most exotic person and fashioned her in a way that captivated me, so I assumed that if I took on her characteristics, I would be captivating too. I told everyone that I was a proven descendant of Queen Nefertiti, and that I had lived in California (though, in reality, I had only lived in boring Pennsylvania) and had spent many hours on the beach with famous actors and actresses who just loved hanging out with my family.

I also grew up without a TV, so when I saw a rare movie or TV show, I saw people who charmed me with their personalities and enchanted me into trying to make anything and everything in my own life just like theirs. I was allowed to go to my Grandfather's to watch the Bionic Woman. I thought she was so beautiful compared to me. I tried to copy her mannerisms and characteristics and took them into the school halls with me. I couldn't open a can of tuna with my bare hands, or hear what was being said a mile away, but I did run fast! (That's a joke.) More importantly, I was impressed by her quiet femininity and the humble way she used her extraordinary gifts. Being more clumsy and awkward myself, I felt she had much to teach me. And I tried to discover <u>something</u> I might have that could be considered extraordinary...I couldn't help myself!

Identity is something every person wrestles with at some time or other in their life. We are all born with the desire to be affirmed and loved. And we seem to come with a tendency to dream big and believe lies. A child becoming Batman is considered 'cute' and it is seen as just a normal part of life...however pretending to be the Bionic Woman as a teenager is not something anyone would ever admit to – because it's not so healthy or wise to be slipping into alter personalities at that age. But how many adults find their identities in "what they do"? It's just another way of putting on a person that isn't really the plain, simple you. As I grew older, I became a PSU student, a teacher-counselor, and a homeschool mom. In each of these seasons of life, I looked to my "job description" as my identity and what I found my security in.

If I find myself identifying with anything more than I identify with Christ, it is an idol. Yes, even being a homeschool mom can be an idol. So many precious young girls today get caught up in comparing themselves with airbrushed models and empty images of what the world calls "beauty". "If I could just look like that, then..._____" You fill in the blank. So they dress a certain way, act a certain way and basically fashion themselves into a living, breathing lie. How this must break the heart of Christ who died that we could find our identity in Him, through His shed blood!

When, as an adult, I finally gave my life to Christ, I knew and felt the change He made in my heart. He changed my striving after trying to find the identity of being ME into being <u>HIS</u>. And it has made all the difference!"

116

None of the things that we look to for happiness or fulfillment other than Jesus will satisfy us, because contentment and joy and love are only found in Him…because He was the one who created these things…and even more than that, He *is* joy, and He *is* love. So how can we expect to find these things apart from Him?

"You make known to me the path of life; in your presence there is fullness of joy; at your right hand are pleasures forevermore." Psalm 16:11

People may tell you that you're crazy and imprudent to follow the Lord's call. Press on. You'll never regret following the Lord.

The Bible actually has quite a lot to say in it about not being distracted by the things of the world, or living our lives for them, and as you read your Bible more, you will come across them. Make sure you underline or highlight them whenever you do, because they will be very helpful to you if you decide to follow God's will for your life and if you decide that you want to serve Him more than you want to chase after any of the things of the world, it will be encouraging and helpful for you to be able to go back over the verses and remember what God has to say about such things. A few verses to get you started are:

"Now there is great gain in godliness with contentment, for we brought nothing into the world, and we cannot take anything out of the world. But if we have food and clothing, with these we will be content. But those who desire to be rich fall into temptation, into a snare, into many senseless and harmful desires that plunge people into ruin and destruction. For the love of money is a root of all kinds of evils. It is through this craving that some have wandered away from the faith and pierced themselves with many pangs. But as for you….flee these things. Pursue righteousness, godliness, faith, love, steadfastness, gentleness." 1 Timothy 6:6-11

"Do not love the world or the things in the world. If anyone loves the world, the love of the Father is not in him. For all that is in the world – the desires of the flesh and the desires of the eyes and pride in possessions – is not from the Father but is from the world. And the world is passing away along with its desires, but whoever does the will of God abides forever." 1 John 2:15-17

I think this is an excellent place to insert a short testimony of my own reasons for giving up the world. I hope it encourages you to take all I've been saying to heart, and to really earnestly pray about it...

Put This To Action:

- What are some of the "worthless" things you have been building your life on? Do you have any dreams or goals which aren't of any eternal value, but are only for selfish reasons? Are you willing to give them up for the Lord?

  _____

  _____

  _____

  _____

  _____

  _____

  _____

  _____

  _____

  _____

  _____

  _____

  _____

  _____

- What are some ways you have chased after "big dreams" in your life?

  _____

  _____

  _____

  _____

  _____

  _____

- Write out how Jesus wants you to think of yourself. How does the example of Jesus' humility affect the way you think of yourself? Do you see the contrast between the two world views of God's humility and the world's prideful self-esteem?:

  _____

  _____

  _____

_____

_____

_____

_____

_____

_____

_____

_____

_____

_____

- What movie or book characters or "role models" have you tried to imitate?

_____

_____

_____

_____

_____

- God wants us to only imitate Jesus. Look up Ephesians 5:1.
- In your personal prayer time, ask God to remove any pride and/or discontentment from your heart, and confess to Him any specific examples He brings to mind.
- Look up Philippians 4:11

Letter 9.5:

Why I Have Given Up the World

1) **The world and all of the things in the world are worthless.**
   - Ephesians 5:11 says, "Take no part in the unfruitful works of darkness, but instead expose them."
     - I have found that all of the things of the world - its glitter and baubles of enticement - are worthless. The TV shows only bring empty and fleeting entertainment and hours of wasted time. The lusts of the world don't satisfy, and only end in pain and disappointment. The mountains of books promising happiness by such-and-such new method only give a short-lived surge of excitement...until you realize that happiness is much harder to grasp than the book made it sound. The blasting music only drowns out the sweet songs of the birds and separates us from our friends and family. The careers we so highly esteem *can* be good and can be used for good, or (and most of the time this is the case:) will sap all energy and time from you as the money you make evaporates and your kids grow up and you're still in the same rut, just living to pay the bills. The gadgets all do the same thing: help you waste more time with things that don't matter – only, the latest ones look cooler, and of course you must spend more money to always have the hottest new gear. The car gets dented or breaks down, and you end up being enslaved to it – sinking more money into it than it's worth for repairs, insurance, gas, upgrades, etc.
     - All the things of this world, when pursued themselves just for the sake of having them or doing them sap all life, joy, and fruitfulness from our lives. They are unfruitful and deadening. It's the never-ending cycle of so many lives, and I have tasted of these things and lived my life in the pursuit of them and found them sorely lacking – as have many others.
     - So why then do so few people turn from them? Why do so many continue to waste their lives always wishing and hoping to do something different and worthwhile, but they remain enslaved to all of the utterly unfruitful works of darkness?
     - Because of fear. Most of these people do not trust God's goodness and ability to sustain them enough to actually take a step like quitting the job or giving up the TV. They are afraid they'll be left

destitute or homeless, or that they'll just be bored, etc. The devil tells us all these things because he knows that the moment we start *actually* seeking the Lord and desiring to serve Him, there will be good fruit…and he wants none of that to happen.

- Also, many people just <u>love</u> the thrill that movies or a new car or a new boyfriend give them, and they don't actually <u>want</u> to give up those things. They assume that spending time with the Lord is boring, or too hard, or that it's just not as "exciting" or "fun" or "rewarding" as reading the latest romance novel or being able to buy the things they want as soon as they want them etc.

2) **The world and all of the things in the world are <u>death</u> for our souls.**

- Romans 8:5-8 says, "For those who live according to the flesh set their minds on the things of the flesh, but those who live according to the Spirit set their minds on the things of the Spirit. For to set the mind on the flesh is death, but to set the mind on the Spirit is life and peace. For the mind that is set on the flesh is hostile to God, for it does not submit to God's law; indeed, it cannot. Those who are in the flesh cannot please God."

- 1 Peter 2:11 says, "Beloved, I urge you as sojourners and exiles to abstain from the passions of the flesh, which wage war against your soul."

  - I didn't realize it at the time that I was participating in many worldly things (and, for the most part, enjoying it), but my soul was shriveling up inside of me. Spending time with God was pretty low on my priority list (though I wouldn't have said it), and there were many days when I never got around to it because I was too busy doing other things, or there were days when I just skimmed over a chapter of the Bible or spent a few minutes in prayer because I felt like it was my "duty". Deep inside, I wanted to be a "good Christian", but was so frustrated that I never seemed to be really "connecting" with God or gaining insight into the Bible. I couldn't seem to understand it. But now, looking back, I can see that it was because I was *so* distracted by *so* many other things – things that seemed "fun" or "important"…movies, books, music, personal goals, dreams, ideas, projects, friends, etc. I couldn't connect with God because I was connected to so many other things. I couldn't live for God rightly because I was living for everything else, and putting everything else first, just like the world said I should. My spirit was dying, and it got to the point where I didn't even <u>try</u> to fight against the passions of my flesh anymore because they had become such a part of me that to kill them seemed like it would have been killing <u>me</u>, myself. And it would have been, because I had become those things and began finding my identity in them instead of in Christ.

3) **The Lord Himself asks us to give up the world in order to serve Him; He knows its perils and dangers. And the world goes directly against everything God is and everything He stands for; we cannot be both friends with God *and* the world.**

- 1 John 2:15-17 says, "Do not love the world or the things in the world. If anyone loves the world, the love of the Father is not in him. For all that is in the world—the desires of the flesh and the desires of the eyes and pride of life—is not from the Father but is from the world. And the world is passing away along with its desires, but whoever does the will of God abides forever."

- Luke 14:33 says, "So therefore, any one of you who does not renounce all that he has cannot be my disciple."

- Luke 18:29-30 says, "And he said to them, 'Truly, I say to you, there is no one who has left house or wife or brothers or parents or children, for the sake of the kingdom of God, who will not receive many times more in this time, and in the age to come eternal life.'"

- James 4:4,8 says, "You adulterous people! Do you not know that friendship with the world is enmity with God? Therefore whoever wished to be a friend of the world makes himself an enemy of God....Draw near to God, and he will draw near to you. Cleanse your hands, you sinners, and purify your hearts, you double-minded."

  - I know Jesus' heart, and that it is completely good. He knows that I can't fully serve Him if I'm distracted by worldly things, and He knows that if worldly things get a grip on me, they will slowly pull me down the way of destruction. I've seen that process happening in my own life already (and the lives of many people I've met), and I do not want to become "lukewarm" or indifferent to the things of God. And, personally, I don't want to have anything to do with anything that is opposed to God or which hurts Him. I'd much rather be *His* friend than a friend of the world, who people of the world highly esteem…and if I have to choose, I'm choosing my Savior and King. I don't want to base my life and efforts around things that will just pass away – I want to invest in eternal things. I want to be Jesus' disciple, and if that means renouncing all of my worldly comforts, then that is what I must do, and nothing less. For the sake of Christ and to be near Him, nothing is too great to surrender. And if He asks it of me, I know it must be for my good, even if I don't fully understand it yet.

4) **What you sow, you will reap.**

- Galatians 6:7-8 says, "Do not be deceived: God is not mocked, for whatever one sows, that will he also reap. For the one who sows to his own flesh will from the flesh reap corruption, but the one who sows to the spirit will from the Spirit reap eternal life."

  - If I am daily imbibing the dregs of worldly media, if I am filling my mind with songs that speak of sinful lusts and passions as being good and acceptable and attractive, if I am watching violent movies with anger and hatred and revenge emanating from them , or if I am watching movies where mocking God or mocking morals or praising immorality or making a joke out of vulgarity is accepted…then what will be the result? This is the result (and I am not speaking hypothetically): My mind will be filled with all of these things all day long, even if/when I go to spend time with the Lord, these things will make themselves comfortable and quite at home in my thoughts. And not only will these things take root in my heart, but they will begin to cloud my sense of God's standards, and I will begin to do, say, and accept things that I wouldn't have before. Things become fuzzy, and sin begins to become acceptable in small (or sometimes not-so-small) doses. If you put garbage into your heart, garbage comes out.

  - But I desire to be wholly God's, to have a pure heart, and to act in a way that is a delight to His heart. I want thoughts and songs and quotes about *Him* and His beauty and holiness and goodness to fill my heart and mind. So then, what must I do, if what I sow, I will also reap? I must turn from all that is contrary to God and a distraction from Him, and instead, begin filling my mind with what is pure and beautiful and worthy of praise in God's eyes. If I want to reap eternal fruit, I must sow to the things that are eternal…and if I don't, I shouldn't be expecting to reap any eternal fruit – it's as simple as that.

5) **Nothing in the world compares to knowing and serving Christ, and seeing the glories of His kingdom!**

- Paul says in Philippians 3:7-9a, "But whatever gain I had, I counted as loss for the sake of Christ. Indeed, I count everything as loss because of the surpassing worth of knowing Christ Jesus my Lord. For his sake I have suffered the loss of all things and count them as rubbish, in order that I may gain Christ and be found in him…"

- Matthew 13:44 says, "'The kingdom of heaven in like a treasure hidden in a field, which a man found and covered up. Then in his joy he goes and sells all that he has and buys that field.'"

  – When you begin to look at everything apart from Christ as rubbish, and gladly give up all that you have and that you had previously treasured in order to gain Christ and the surpassing worth of knowing Him and the beauties and delights of His kingdom, it just all makes sense. It makes sense when you have tasted of the fullness of Christ. It makes sense when you have gotten a glimpse of the treasures of His kingdom and the Celestial City. When you have drunk of the pure, clear, cool, refreshing springs of Living Water, how can you go back to the slimy, polluted cesspool of the world and drink from it?? And why would you want to? I have come to see and know for a certain that the glories of Christ far surpass any shallow, man-made adventure film or mystery novel or popular band or pile of paper money. None of it comes even close to the beauty and life and joy found in my Lord – and even on my worst day, His companionship is sweet beyond words, and I gladly leave all of it behind if I might gain more of Him, and even if that were the only reason, it would be enough.

6) **I have been preceded by amazing men and women of God who have given all – even their very lives – for the Lord. Who am I to think I can obtain this treasure of greatest worth by clinging to all my fleshly desires and just "sliding in" to heaven? Let it not be so!**

- Hebrews 12:1-4 says, "Therefore, since we are surrounded by so great a cloud of witnesses, let us also lay aside every weight and sin which clings so closely, and let us run with endurance the race that is set before us, looking to Jesus, the founder and perfecter of our faith, who for the joy that was set before him endured the cross, despising the shame, and is seated at the right hand of the throne of God. Consider him who endured from sinners such hostility against himself, so that you may not grow weary or fainthearted. In your struggle against sin you have not yet resisted to the point of shedding your blood."

- How can it be that so many great men and women have gone before me – both in Biblical times (many who are listed in Hebrews 11) and throughout more recent years (think of the martyrs of the early church, the martyrs in China, Adoniram Judson, Mary Slessor, Gladys Aylward, the Goforths, Brother Yun, etc., etc.) who have given up everything for the sake of the Lord, for the sake of the gospel, and for the sake of their eternal treasure....and yet *we* think we can have the Lord and all of our idols and personal comforts too; that we can have an earthly mound of treasure and fulfilled desires and still expect to find an eternal inheritance waiting for us, that we really cared nothing about until our dying day? These men and women have given up homes, families, comfort, personal dreams, worldly esteem, health, time, and even their *lives* for the Lord, and in order to not forsake His name, and in order to make His name known to others…and yet, we expect to be able to slide into heaven still holding onto our flatscreen TV and our perfect careers, where we have made a name for ourselves in the world.

- What does God think when he sees us whimpering over not being able to give up our Twilight books, or our favorite pop band to serve Him and/or spend more time with Him, when He sees all the martyrs and those who, at this very moment are being tortured because they love Him so much that they would give up anything and everything before they would ever even think of renouncing Him? And yet, we renounce Him for far lesser things every day. And what about the great cloud of witnesses who had the faith to trust God and do His will no matter what the personal cost was – what do they think when they watch us clinging to every last straw of the world that we can? Their hearts must be torn in pieces, because they have loved the Lord with such a deep love, that to see our pettiness must cause them great pain.

- For this reason, I count nothing too much to give for the sake of following the Lord.

- "And those who are wise shall shine like the brightness of the sky above; and those who turn many to righteousness, like the stars forever and ever." (Daniel 12:3)
  - There may be many who argue against me and who say these things aren't really important or necessary to follow Christ…or those who simply love the world too much to even consider what I'm saying as true. But as for me, this is the <u>only</u> way. The Lord is my life, and serving Him is all that matters to me in this life. He alone I have chosen to serve, and I, by His grace and strength, will not go back or turn aside to the world. How can I when I have beheld His beauty? I will not look back.

My husband's family (The Skys) has put together a commitment for people to take who have come to understand that the world and everything in it is empty, and that seeking the Lord above everything else is the most valuable and important thing in life. It's just a short commitment that you can print out and sign (to make it official, and to remind you that it's important) which says that you want to take a fast from worldly movies, books, music, pasttimes, etc., in order to spend that time with the Lord instead, and to get untangled from all of the influences of the world, which will eventually drag you down the path of destruction if you don't run from them. The commitment is for one year, which isn't a terribly long time, though it may seem like it at first, especially when all of those worldly things you really want to do seem so appealing. You can also begin by just "signing up" for half of a year at first, to try it out (though I don't recommend going any shorter than that, because it takes several months just to be able to get completely untangled from the grip of all of these worldly, sinful things; they don't let go of us easily). You can find the commitment in Appendix A! You should really seriously think about this, because it is actually a very important step in being able to grow closer to the Lord, and serve Him.

If you decide to take the commitment, I'd love to know about it! And I'm also here if you have any questions, or are struggling to keep the commitment, or if you need prayer. Feel free to write to me, and I will try to get back to you as soon as I can. My email address is: unshakablegirls@gmail.com (make sure you double-check the spelling before you send it).

Put This To Action:

- What are you going to do about this?

_____

_____

_____

_____

_____

_____

_____

_____

_____

_____

Letter 10:

Don't Not Do Anything

Dear Every-girl,

I am going to make this a shorter letter, and more to-the-point, because I don't think it requires a whole lot of explanation, because Jesus is pretty to-the-point about it. The point of this letter is to show you that there is an importance and need for you to put to action the things you have been learning as you've read through this book, and as the Holy Spirit has been teaching you...and that God actually requires it of you. Now that you have heard the truth, you have the responsibility to choose what you're going to do with that knowledge; either ignore it and go your own way, or put it into action bit by bit, day by day...to let it affect you and the change way you live your life. What does God say about it?

First, I will share with you a parable that Jesus told:

"For it [Jesus' coming] will be like a man going on a journey, who called his servants and entrusted to them his property. To one he gave five talents, to another two, to another one, to each according to his ability. Then he went away. He who had received the five talents went at once and traded with them, and he made five talents more. So also he who had the two talents made two talents more. But he who had received the one talent went and dug in the ground and hid his master's money. Now after a long time the master of those servants came and settled accounts with them. And he who had received the five talents came forward, bringing five talents more, saying, 'Master, you delivered to me five talents; here I have made five talents more.' His master said to him, 'Well done, good and faithful servant. You have been faithful over a little; I will set you over much. Enter into the joy of your master.' And he also who had the two talents came forward, saying, 'Master, you delivered to me two talents; here I have made two talents more.' His master said to him, 'Well done, good and faithful servant. You have been faithful over a little; I will set you over much. Enter into the joy of your master.' He also who had received the one talent came forward, saying, 'Master, I knew you to be a hard man, reaping where you did not sow, and gathering where you scattered no seed, so I was afraid, and I went and hid your talent in the ground. Here you have what is yours.' But his master answered him, 'You wicked and slothful servant! You knew that I reap where I have not sown and gather where I scattered no seed? Then you ought to have

invested my money with the bankers, and at my coming I should have received what was my own with interest. So take the talent from him and give it to him who has the ten talents. For to everyone who has will more be given, and he will have an abundance. But from the one who has not, even what he has will be taken away. And cast the worthless servant into the outer darkness. In that place there will be weeping and gnashing of teeth.' Matthew 25:14-30

The talents (a sum of money in Biblical times) each of the servants received have been compared to many things over the years and in many different sermons and teachings. But, for this letter, I am going to compare the talents to knowledge. So put yourself in the place of one of those servants in the parable. God has given you knowledge about things that maybe you hadn't even thought of before. He has shown you with scriptures and much love His heart of concern for you. He has placed this gift into your hands today...and the question is...what will you do with it? Will you squander and throw away these things you have read and learned, and be willing to stand before Jesus, the King of Kings at the end of your life, and have Him say to you, "You wicked servant"? Or will you take these things to heart, learning from them, and begin to ask the Lord to help you apply them to your own life, and have them multiply for eternal good in your life...and will the Lord say to you, "Well done, good and faithful servant"?

Next, James 1:21-25 says, *"Therefore put away all filthiness and rampant wickedness and receive with meekness the implanted word, which is able to save your souls. But be <u>doers</u> of the word, and not hearers only, deceiving yourselves. For if anyone is a hearer of the word and not a doer, he is like a man who looks intently at his natural face in a mirror. For he looks at himself and goes away and at once forgets what he was like. <u>But the one who looks into the perfect law, the law of liberty, and perseveres, being no hearer who forgets but a doer who acts, he will be blessed in his doing.</u>"*

This is a pretty straight-forward passage of scripture. Through it, God is telling us that, if we hear the truth of His word and don't act on it, we are deceiving ourselves. It is like going to years of piano recitals and lessons and telling people that you can play the piano...but all the while, you have never actually touched a piano before, and if you did, it would not be the sweet sound you are hoping for. Playing the piano means that you have to take all that you've learned and put it into practice…and practice…and practice…and practice some more.

In a similar way, if you say you are a Christian, but you are choosing to ignore some of God's commands, or if you just aren't putting effort into living as Jesus asks us to, and you go along assuming it will kind of just happen overnight…you will be disappointed to find that you aren't receiving the blessings of truly walking in God's ways. *But*, if you *do* act on it, and continue to persevere in changing and growing closer to God…it w*ill* happen, and you will be greatly blessed to look back some day several years down the road, and see all that God has done *in* and *through* and *for* you…and then you will be able to see a clearer picture of the great value of acting on His commands. As I mentioned before, you will never regret serving the Lord.

And last, Jesus says these unexpected words, *"But he answered them, 'My mother and my brothers are those who hear the word of God and do it.'"* Luke 8:21

These words are surprising, but also super sweet. Jesus Himself is saying that if we are those who take heed of His words and act on them, He actually considers us to be his family – not just figuratively speaking, but His *actual* family. To think that Jesus Himself – the King of All, who has always been, and always will be – would consider *us* weak little humans His very own family is an incredible thought, and a promise straight from His lips. And that by itself is reason enough for me to desire to act on His words. His heart is so good.

As you begin taking action on the things in this book, as you begin spending more time with the Lord, and begin to want to serve Him in any way you can, an important first step to take is to just get out and serve God and serve others!

Are you wondering how you can possibly serve the Lord? It can sometimes be very easy to begin thinking that there isn't really much that you can actually do for God, especially if you are young. First, the best thing to keep in mind is to start small but pray big. This means that you don't immediately have to go out and be a well-known evangelist and lead hundreds of people to the Lord. It also means that you don't have to immediately go out to Africa and live among the natives there by yourself. What it does mean is that you can begin praying and asking God to provide opportunities for you to serve Him and to tell other people about Him, and praying for the boldness to do whatever He asks…and then doing it! And it can be anything from talking about Jesus and how He has changed you with your friends, to leaving tracts in bathrooms and places you go, to posting notes on facebook about what God is teaching you and praying that He causes the right people to read them, to starting to read the Bible with a couple of friends (and reading it out-loud in a fast-food restaurant or a coffee shop can be an awesome opportunity to share the gospel with people around you), etc. But if you ask God, He will give you even more great ideas!!

One last note though: I realize that we are weak and sinful, and we can't act on God's words without help…and even if we do succeed to some degree, we will almost always mess up and fail from time to time. In these cases and at all times we must just continually come to the Lord in prayer and ask for His strength and help…and as we humble ourselves and ask Him…He will indeed help us. And day by day, one thing at a time, He will begin to change us to be more like Him. And we will begin to notice Him giving us boldness in areas where we were scared before, and faith in areas that we doubted. God is very good at taking our weaknesses and making them into strengths.

Put This To Action:

- What are the "talents" God has given to you through this book and through His Word?

  _____
  _____
  _____
  _____
  _____
  _____

- What are some ways you can practice serving the Lord this week? Write at least 5, and then <u>do</u> them. Ask for God's blessing and guidance on each of the things you do.

  _____
  _____
  _____
  _____

- What is an idea for how you can get out and serve the Lord that wasn't mentioned in this chapter?

  _____
  _____
  _____

- Write down some of your weaknesses and, next to them, their opposites (Example: fear = faith and boldness). Start praying that God will overcome your weaknesses and begin growing their opposites in you as strengths.

  _____ = _____
  _____ = _____
  _____ = _____
  _____ = _____
  _____ = _____
  _____ = _____
  _____ = _____

139

Letter 11:

Why Should Any Of This Affect You?

Dear Every-girl,

So why should any of what I've said in this book affect you? Why do all of these things matter? Well, it is because we all, if we are honest, have the desire to do something with our lives that is meaningful, and a good use of the years we have been given to live, and something that will make a lasting impact. However, because so many people don't know their Creator, they wander through life trying to find happiness and fulfillment....but they can never find those things apart from the Lord. And why is that?

God created us to be wonderful creatures, full of life and beauty and purpose. His original plan was for us to be able to spend all of our time with Him, in His presence, just enjoying being with Him and learning all of the things He wanted to teach us. Just think – spending time with the God who always existed and always will exist, Who is perfectly pure and just and humble, and Who created every particle in the entire universe would be such an incredible privilege! (No other "god" known to man ever wanted to just spend time with the people on earth just because he loved being with them...and yet, that is what our God wanted!)

So why is there all the corruption, and pain, and brokenness in the world then, if we were supposed to have a beautiful, innocent world full of joy and peace? It is because we rebelled against God and His plans, and we thought He was holding back something from us that we deserved...and so, we have disobeyed Him, and in doing so, sin has entered into the world and consumed each heart, so that no one on earth is free from sin. Romans 3:23 says, *"...for all have sinned and fall short of the glory of God..."*. We all disobey God's laws continually, and are continually reaping the consequences. Our God is a just God, and He must punish sin, though He does not delight in it...but if He did not punish sin, the wicked would prosper and the innocent would suffer. Thus, we have all separated *ourselves* from God's presence.

So if we have all committed terrible crimes against the pure, holy, and just God, and we have caused ourselves to be separated from His presence, and to be slated for eternal punishment...is there any hope? Can our lives ever be rescued? You may be surprised to learn that the only thing separating us from forgiveness and lives that are full of God's joy and blessing is…*our own pride.* Yep. That is the main thing that keeps millions of people from experiencing freedom in Christ, and instead, they stay wrapped in chains in the dark dungeon of the world's enticements. No one really wants to admit that they have done anything wrong and that they need help. We all want to think that we are good people, and that because our parents are Christians, or because we have lots of friends and everyone likes us, or because we do nice things for people, or because we aren't as bad as so-and-so, we don't need any help. But the truth is that good deeds don't pay the price for our sins, which is an incredibly high price – so high that none of us could actually ever pay it. And we can't compare ourselves to anyone but God Himself, because His standards are absolute perfection…and no one on earth is able to be perfect…so even if we think we are good compared to someone else, we are still wicked according to God's standards. So what is the hope? God sent His Son, Jesus, Who is also completely perfect, to pay the death penalty that we owed for our sins (He was the only one who could pay the penalty, because He is the only one Who has never sinned, and therefore, He didn't owe any penalty Himself – because a guilty person can't rescue someone else, because they are guilty themselves; the rescue has to be from someone who hasn't broken the law)…and because of this, Jesus has offered to us forgiveness of our sins, and a changed heart! Romans 6:23 says, *"For the wages of sin is death, but the free gift of God is eternal life in Christ Jesus our Lord."* And if we accept this gift, when God looks at us, He sees the perfection of Jesus covering us like a robe, instead of our own weaknesses and failures. And after Jesus came to die on the cross for our sins, God raised Him from the dead 3 days later, breaking the power of sin and death!

The one thing that we must do to receive this gift of God is to humble ourselves and repent of our sins…and many people can't get past that one simple requirement, because they don't want to admit that they are sinners, and that they actually deserve the punishment of God. However, when someone sees clearly that they *have* sinned and broken God's law, and that they do, in fact, deserve to be punished…and when that person is willing to come before the Lord and admit to Him that they have sinned, and to genuinely say that they are sorry for their sins…and when they are willing to ask God to forgive their sins and to take them away and to give them a new heart; when that person accepts Jesus' sacrifice on the cross as the only way that they can be saved and escape the curse of sin that is on the world, then God looks on them with tenderness and love instead of judgment…and He will actually completely forgive that person's sins, and begin to make their hearts brand new. 1 John 1:9 says, *"If we confess our sins He is faithful and just to forgive us and cleanse us from all unrighteousness."* And Romans 10:13 says, *"Whoever calls on the name of the Lord will be saved."* And again, John 5:24 says, *"Truly, truly I say to you, he who hears My [Jesus'] word and believes in Him who sent me has eternal life and does not come into judgment, but has passed out of death into life."*

This book was written to show you how you can escape the emptiness of the world…and that is through cultivating a real, living relationship with Jesus Christ. But it can't be cultivated unless it begins here, with this simple act of humbling yourself, and repenting. And then, every time you find yourself messing up and sinning again (it will happen), just coming humbly to God again, and saying you're sorry and asking for His forgiveness and help again. It's a daily (sometimes hourly) practice that will change your life…and it starts here.

Do you want to be set free from being a slave to your sins? Do you want to be able to actually have freedom, and joy like you have never known before? Do you want to give your life to the Lord, for His use? Do you want to be His child, and to dwell with Him forever? If you are ready to receive the Lord into your life, I recommend either asking someone you know who is also a Christian to pray with you, or going into your room, closing the door, and just start talking to the Lord about all of these things. Below I've written out a simple prayer which is just a guideline – you can pray it word-for-word, or you can read over it, and then pray about the things in it in your own words. It doesn't really matter exactly what words you use, because God looks at your heart. I do, however, suggest praying out loud, because there's something really special about speaking directly to the Lord. Romans 10:9-10 says, *"…because, if you confess with your mouth that Jesus is Lord and believe in your heart that God raised him from the dead, you will be saved. For with the heart one believes and is justified, and with the mouth one confesses and is saved."*

Lord Jesus, I come before you today to admit that I have sinned against You and broken Your commands. I am sorry Lord for all of my sins [and you can go on to confess specific ones that Jesus brings to your mind], and I'm sorry for breaking Your heart, and for rebelling against Your good desires. I believe that You have died on the cross to take the punishment that I deserved, and that You rose from the dead, breaking the power of sin and death! I ask that You would forgive all of my sins, and that You would remove them from me and clean my heart out from them.   Thank-You for forgiving me, and for making my heart new! I ask You to be the Lord of my life, and to be in control, because I can't live in a way that is pleasing to You on my own. I pray that You would change me, and make me into Your child, and who loves You more than anything else, and who You can use to bring forth eternal fruit. Thank-You for dying so that I could be free! Amen!

And you can also ask for the Holy Spirit, like I talked about in the 2nd letter in this book; in the same way you just prayed for salvation, ask Jesus to fill you with His Holy Spirit, so that you can resist the temptations of the devil, so that you can understand God's Word better, and so that you can serve the Lord better…and He will!

Now let someone know…tell your family, tell a Christian friend, tell a pastor, and/or send me a note to tell me that you've just become a Christian…it would really bless me to know…since this whole book is because I care about you. (Again, my email address is: unshakablegirls@gmail.com)

Appendix A

Fellowship of the Unashamed Member

By the grace of God, I willingly accept a commitment to abstain from the pleasures and pursuits of this world in order to seek the Lord whole heartedly for the period of one year. I purpose to join with other believers to "seek the things above where Christ is seated at the right hand of the Father" by "setting [my] mind on the things above, not on the things that are on the earth."

FORSAKING THE THINGS OF THE FLESH

"Do not be deceived, God is not mocked; for whatever a man sows that he will also reap. For the one who sows to his own flesh shall from the flesh reap corruption, but the one who sows to the Spirit shall from the Spirit reap eternal life." I desire to stop sowing to the flesh which endangers my soul and therefore commit to forsaking TV, worldly entertainment, deadening secular input of all sorts, video games, unnecessary and ungodly computer input, drugs, alcohol, and all fleshly indulgence. I use for my guide the words of Psalm 101:
"I will walk within my house in the integrity of my heart. I will set no worthless thing before my eyes; I hate the work of those who fall away; It shall not fasten it's grip on me."

SOWING TO THE SPIRIT

It is my intent to use this time to earnestly seek God. I commit to a program of regular Bible reading and private prayer. I desire to enter into close communion with the Living God that I might begin to see the fruit of the Spirit manifested in my life. I commit to listening only to edifying music and enjoying uplifting entertainment. I use the words of Jesus in John 15 as a guide; "I am the vine, you are the branches; he who abides in Me and I in him, he bears much fruit; for apart from me you can do nothing." I desire to become a fruitful worker for the Kingdom of God and I am willing to pay the price of staying attached to the Vine Himself. It is the greatest joy and truest satisfaction to embrace the cross of Christ in order to follow in His footsteps.

GREATER LOVE HAS NO MAN

"If you abide in Me and my words abide in you, ask whatever you wish and it shall be done for you. By this is My Father glorified, that you bear much fruit and so prove to be my disciples." I take as my inspiration the commitment Jeremiah lived by which was to make it a point to speak to a least one person each day about the love of God. In this commitment I am able to truly enter the fellowship of the unashamed.

GOD'S GRACE

I realize that I am in no way entering a relationship with God based on my works, but I desire to obey His word "If by the Spirit you are putting to death the deeds of the body you will live." and "Do not be conformed to the world but be transformed by the renewing of your mind" and "abstaining from worldly lusts which wage war against your soul." I openly confess that I have no power in myself to adhere to this commitment, but look to the sustaining power of God and His grace alone to pursue this course. To God alone be the power and glory.

Member_____   Date_____

Appendix B

40 Biblical Qualities of Manhood

(Take note that this list can also be used to evaluate your OWN life; are you the kind of person a godly guy like this would want to marry? Are there things on this list that are not displayed in your own life?)

1. Is he a Christian (He <u>must</u> be)? Does he fear the Lord? Job 1:1.
2. Is he just? Matthew 1:19.
3. Is he blameless and upright? Job 1:1.
4. Does he <u>turn away</u> from evil? Job 1:1.
5. Has he purposed not to defile himself? Daniel 1:8.
6. Does he hone his God-given skills? 1 Samuel 16:18.
7. Is he prudent in his speech? 1 Samuel 16:18.
8. Is he unafraid to stand up for what he believes? 1 Samuel 16:18.
9. Is he a man of valor/chivalry? 1 Samuel 16:18.
10. Is the Lord with him? Is the blessing of the Lord evident in his life? 1 Samuel 16:18.
11. Do others think/speak highly of him? Is he a man of good presence? 1 Samuel 16:18, Acts 6:3.
12. Is he filled with the Holy Spirit? Acts 6:3, Ephesians 6: 17-18.
13. Is he full of wisdom? Acts 6:3.
14. Is he full of grace? Acts 6:8.
15. Has he put on the whole armor of God? Ephesians 6:10-19.
    a. Is he truthful? Eph. 6:14,
    b. Is he righteous? Eph. 6:14,
    c. Is he ready to meet God? Eph. 6:15,
    d. Does he have faith? Eph. 6:16,
    e. Does he <u>often</u> speak with God? Eph 6:18,
    f. Is he alert with perseverance, making supplication (praying) for all the saints? Eph. 6:18,
    g. Does he boldly proclaim the gospel? Ephesians 6: 19.
16. Does he display Christ's love? Ephesians 6:25, Colossians 3:14.
17. Is he humble? Ephesians 4:2.
18. Is he gentle? Ephesians 4:2.

19. Is he patient? Ephesians 4:2, 2 Timothy 2:24.
20. Is Christ and his Word (as the Head) the first source of guidance for him? 1 Corinthians 11:3.
21. Is he faithful in all he does- including teaching others? 2 Timothy 2:2.
22. Is he kind to everyone? 2 Timothy 2:24.
23. Does he correct with gentleness? 2 Timothy 2:25.
24. Is he committed to not divorce? 1 Corinthians 7: 10-11.
25. Is he not overly concerned with outward appearances? 1 Samuel 16:7, Romans 12:16.
26. Is he well-spoken? 1 Timothy 4:12, Colossians 4:6.
27. Is he committed to purity? 1 Timothy 4:12.
28. Does he pursue godly activities? Is he the same person alone that he is in a group? 1 Timothy 4:12.
29. Is he diligent/making the most of his time? Ephesians 5:15.
30. Does he not quit something without a good reason? Is he industrious/a hard worker? Luke 9:62.
31. Is he self-sacrificing? Romans 12:1.
32. Does he know how to discern the will of God? Romans 12:2.
33. Is he compassionate? Colossians 3:12.
34. Does he repay evil with good? Romans 12:14-21.
35. Does he honor his whole family? Exodus 20:12.
36. Does he walk in integrity? Proverbs 11:3, 10:11.
37. Is he humble? Does he accept correction well? Proverbs 12:1, 13:1.
38. Does he seek out truth for himself? Proverbs 14:15.
39. Does he use his gifts and talents to serve others? Is he a humble and willing servant? 1 Peter 4:10, Galations 5:13.
40. Is he self-controlled? Gal.5:23.

Yet, someone who had not attained 'perfection' in all of these qualities, but was earnestly desiring them, and striving to attain them, with God's help...I would consider that person for marriage. That is, perhaps, the most essential quality.

Find Tai Sophia's blog online at:

www.beggarlybouquet.com

Get in touch with Tai at:

unshakablegirls@gmail.com

Write to Tai at:

162 Harding Creek Road

Clinton, PEI Canada

C0B 1M0

Find out more about the Bible School Tai attended, and her family's ministry at:

www.theskys.org

Find more copies of this book on Amazon.com